Praise for

HOOKED

'Brave, poignant and very moving.
This book will change lives.'
Jamie Redknapp

'A courageous, emotional and vitally important book.'
Jeff Stelling

'A fantastic book . . . a remarkable read.'
Richard Madeley, *Good Morning Britain*

'Brave . . . visceral . . . a brilliant, brilliant read . . .
I would recommend this book to everyone.'
Nihal Arthanayake, BBC Radio 5 Live

'Even when baring his soul, Paul Merson is
entertainingly fluent in the language of football.
The Merse's new book, *Hooked*, is frank,
sometimes funny, often horrifying.'
Irish Examiner

'So honest . . . everybody should read *Hooked*
to understand what anybody in this situation
has been through.'
Susanna Reid, *Good Morning Britain*

Also by Paul Merson

Rock Bottom

Hero and Villain

How Not to be a Professional Footballer

PAUL MERSON

WITH ROB BAGCHI

HOOKED

Addiction and the
Long Road to Recovery

HEADLINE

First published in 2021 by
HEADLINE PUBLISHING GROUP

First published in paperback in 2022 by
HEADLINE PUBLISHING GROUP

3

Cataloguing in Publication Data is available from the British Library

ISBN 978 1 4722 8256 9

Designed and typeset by EM&EN
Printed and bound in Great Britain by Clays Ltd, Elcograf S.p.A.

Headline's policy is to use papers that are natural, renewable and recyclable
products and made from wood grown in well-managed forests and other
controlled sources. The logging and manufacturing processes are expected
to conform to the environmental regulations of the country of origin.

HEADLINE PUBLISHING GROUP
An Hachette UK Company
Carmelite House
50 Victoria Embankment
London EC4Y 0DZ

www.headline.co.uk
www.hachette.co.uk

To Kate, the one person
who truly understands me.

CONTENTS

INTRODUCTION:

THE CLOWN OF A MILLION FACES

May 1998. It's a lovely warm Sunday afternoon at Highbury in north London, home of Arsenal and my home, too, for thirteen years.

I'm not playing. I left Arsenal for Middlesbrough the summer before but I'm watching the game on TV. At the Riverside, we've just beaten Oxford in our last game of the season and now we're going up to the top flight. Down in London, Arsenal are 3–0 ahead and in a minute they will be crowned Premier League champions. Steve Bould has come on as a late substitute and scoops the ball over the Everton defence for another former member of 'The Tuesday Club'.

I don't even know what Tony Adams is doing there, galloping in isolation towards the North Bank. I'm not sure he does either but there he is, my good mate Tone, taking a touch on his hip. He has played about a million games and never done that before. Just him and the keeper now. The ball sits up beautifully and he rifles a left-foot half-volley across the goalie and into the far corner. The North Bank goes up. I've known him half my life and didn't even think he could kick with his left foot, but some things are meant to be. He turns, stands there and closes his eyes with a great big smile on his face. He's been sober coming up for two years. In a few seconds he'll be mobbed by the lads – Wrighty and Ray, Dennis and Bouldy. But before they get to him, that moment, the stillness, with his arms spread wide, eyes shut, beaming, is iconic. It ought to be a poster. It's the purest image of recovery I know.

Mine's a bit different. I first confronted my addictions eighteen months before Tone. He was inspired in some ways by me, as he'd tell you himself, when he acknowledged he, too, was an alcoholic. But my recovery, like my addictions, has been messier. I've had long spells of being sober, managed to resist the compulsion to gamble for periods of various lengths and have gone nearly three decades without wanting to go anywhere near cocaine, the third addictive illness which brought me to my knees in barely ten months in 1994. Coke took me to the brink of madness and I'm certain, if I'd carried on, that I wouldn't be here now.

I've had my moments of serenity, but no picture as public and perfect as Tone's: the birth of my kids, my wedding to Kate and one or two when I was still a footballer, especially the night we won promotion at Portsmouth, the most fulfilling season of my career when I was well enough to enjoy most of it. I'm well now, too. I'm the happiest I've ever been in my whole life and I don't have anything apart from my family and a job I love. I've lost millions and millions of pounds to the bookies, lost houses, blown my entire pension and almost destroyed my self-respect. But I've been off the booze for more than two years and not had a bet for a year. The fog in my mind is finally clearing.

The longer I'm sober, the more clearly I see and think. An image of my recovery would be more personal and low-key. It would be me, struggling but utterly absorbed in putting together a doll's house for my daughter, Sienna. I'm useless at DIY, flat packs and all that. In the past, I would have got someone in to do it for me or it would have stayed in the box for a year. Not this time. I can't say I'll ever love doing it, but once I'd finished I had a genuine sense of satisfaction.

We hosted a barbecue last summer. Nothing special in that, is there? But it was for me, because at the age of fifty-two it was something I'd never done before. I was the bloke who went to other people's barbecues. I would have a laugh and a good drink all afternoon and way beyond, knocking back bottle after bottle long after most people had left, having batted off God knows how many requests from my wife to call it a night. Once I'd started drinking, I didn't know how to stop. Now I'm manning the grill. All I've wanted my entire life is to be normal – take the kids to the park, sit in the garden, Sunday roast – and be someone my family could rely on. Normality is the ultimate for me. And every day I'm getting there.

You may have seen me play for Arsenal and England, Middlesbrough, Aston Villa and Pompey and scoff at the idea that I suffered from crippling anxiety and shyness. I'm made up of a lorryload of contradictions, because playing in front of big, raucous crowds never fazed me. I would never cheat by shirking the opportunity to hit the killer pass. If I saw it I played it, even if it hadn't come off five times before. I've taken a penalty for England in a World Cup shootout and it never entered my mind to be scared. On the field, I was fine. I was safe. But off it, I never wanted to live inside my own head. My addictions were all about chasing away the doubt and fear of everyday life, and altering the way I felt.

Drink helped me to be the clown, to have a million faces. I could go into a place and people would never know there was something wrong. There's a bit of an art to that, but it's a dark art and no good for you. You're suppressing all the emotions instead of talking about them. I didn't want to be that person – shitting in Perry Groves' pillowcase, or sitting on top of a limo in Washington DC pissed out of my mind and refusing to come down as the England manager begged me to behave, or trashing Gus Caesar's hotel room and provoking him almost to the point of murdering me, or countless other escapades – I wanted to be Alan Smith or David Rocastle. I wanted to be a family man. I could often handle not drinking but whenever I did, the first gulp would bring an irresistible urge to keep going until the bitter end.

I started gambling at sixteen. My first month's pay packet on the YTS scheme at Arsenal was gone in 10 minutes at William Hill. A compulsion to bet has been a constant throughout my adult life. Sometimes I've been able to steer clear, but even when I was at my best as a footballer in five alcohol-free years at Villa and Pompey, I was losing millions. By the time I appeared in the ITV show *Harry's Heroes* and broke down in tears when talking about its devastating effect on my family's life, I'd been through residential rehab twice but I feared I could never break its hold on me.

It's a truly hideous illness and I wouldn't wish it on anyone.

I did stop betting after filming the programme. I went back to Gamblers Anonymous after ages away and gradually I began to get better. The TV programme was important in that. You can go out, get drunk and lose your money and you forget about it after a while. But to have it on film, how bad the gambling and drinking were, gives you a true, permanent record of what rock bottom looks and feels like. To see yourself in the grip of it, at death's door on the telly, with no self-worth and overwhelmed by guilt, is liberating but traumatic. I've been there loads, wanting to kill myself enough times over my gambling, but I kept going back to it. I can see how people go mad. It's horrible. You know you can't win, you know the end point is you with nothing left, hollowed out, a total wreck, but the voice won't be silenced. It says, 'This time. This time we'll do it right.'

I did go back. In the first lockdown last year, I lost everything. There were no physical GA meetings and I didn't look after myself properly. I lost our deposit to buy a house, lost the lot. I'd saved and saved since giving up betting the previous year so we could move from renting and get our own home. And it went before I could catch my breath. I couldn't handle the lockdown, I couldn't see a way out of despair or fight off the fatalistic feelings. I was thinking, when's this all going to stop? Are we all going to die? Everything felt bleak and terrifying, so I did what I had always done to fill my mind with different thoughts. I had a bet, then another and another until I was on the floor.

The shame is mind-blowing.

•

This book is, of course, for people who love football, fans of all the clubs I played for and those of Walsall, too, the club I managed and the only real regret of my career. It's for all of you who watch *Soccer Saturday*.

But I really want it to chime with people who can't get out from under their addictions, for those who think they're bad people because they don't know they're ill. You're not alone: we're not crackpots, we're not weak, we're not evil, we're not failures. And it isn't about mental strength. Illnesses aren't cured by determination. You can't beat diarrhoea with willpower. Meetings, treatment and talking are the things that help you get well and because of them, that's where I am now.

All I hope is that one person picks up this book and thinks, 'I gamble like him or drink like him and he feels exactly like I feel.' Writing this has helped me come to terms with the traumatic effects of addiction on thirty-five years of my life, to see with new eyes the things I did through choice or compulsion and how I became the man

I am today. If this book manages to save just one person, it would be the best thing I've ever done in my life. Because it could have a roll-on effect: if they're married and have kids, then the message can go through the generations, not just affecting an individual but maybe fifty people.

What you do as an addict is beat yourself up all the time. The more you beat yourself up, telling yourself you're horrible, the more you turn to drink, drugs, gambling to escape from that certainty that you're a bad person. The worst thing about being an addict in the full throes of addiction is not knowing what makes you act the way you do. When you do understand, believe me it becomes a lot easier. Before that the self-hatred will grind you down, and because no one wants to feel that bad all the time, the one way you think will get you out of that place is through the things that put you there in the first place. It's a cycle and you can only start to get better when you know you are one of hundreds of thousands of people affected by this exhausting illness.

Some days are still hard, but now I recognise they're really no different to anyone else's bad days. I'm not that special. Every morning, I have a little quiet time to think and pray for patience and for my selfishness not to affect me today. At night, I go to bed and put my head on the pillow and appreciate that it's a miracle that I haven't had a bet or a drink. It might sound extreme but after thirty-seven years of living with my addictive personality, it's not. It's a miracle. You wouldn't realise what a big thing that is for me. It is like winning the Tour de France for a cyclist.

I know it's not over. After all this time, it can't be. For all of those like me, our addictions are out there doing press-ups, just waiting. Ask me to tell you that I'll never have another bet or drink and I couldn't do it. But today I'm well and that's good enough for me.

1

LAND OF THE GIANTS

I can't really remember a time before addiction.

I can though remember most of what happened in my childhood. I grew up in a flat in Harlesden in north-west London, which we shared with my auntie and uncle and their three children, and then Northolt, much further out west, where we moved into our own council house when I was ten. But I can't remember what the *absence* of addiction felt like, what life was like free from obsessing and scheming about betting.

It might not have been gambling that was ruling my emotions as a kid but my head was not in a peaceful place. I was not a happy-go-lucky boy. I was the eldest of four, part of a large, close-knit extended family. My dad, Fred, was a coalman. It was a tough, demanding job and he used to come home with his hands all beaten up from hauling the sacks. My mum, June, was an office cleaner for Remploy at Staples Corner – another hard job. I'm full of respect for the way they'd come home on dark, winter nights and put dinner on the table. There's more pressure in doing that than there ever is on a football pitch.

I think the contrast between seeing what they had to do to earn money and what I did was part of the problem in my early days of gambling. I was outside in the fresh air, playing football, the best game in the world. By the time I was in the first team at Arsenal, training was short and sharp, barely a four-hour working day there and back. I was getting paid bundles and I couldn't justify earning that sort of money. It had no sense of value. So when I lost it, it didn't hurt too much because I wasn't having to go to work at 6 a.m. on a building site, or down the mine, to earn some more. At the start, it didn't affect me when I lost because deep down I thought I shouldn't be getting it anyway. I'd say to myself, 'What am I getting paid that much for?'

It really was 'easy come, easy go' at the beginning, in a way it never had been or could be for my parents. I was very attached to both, particularly my dad, and I didn't like being away from him. I was a nervous child, frightened of all sorts of things, absolutely petrified of dogs for one, and sensitive to the stresses of family life caused by money troubles and unemployment. I suffered from separation anxiety, among other things. I'd wet the bed a lot and would suck my thumb as a comfort thing past the age of ten.

My dad was a good footballer in his youth and had been on QPR's books after he came out of the army but didn't get into the first team. He still played on Saturday afternoons and when his mates called for him, I'd get in a right state, trying to persuade him to stay with me instead. There'd be tears and I'd be upset until he came home. I just loved being in his company, going out with him on his rounds at the weekend, and would look for reassurance that he'd be around most nights. 'You're not going out tonight, are you Dad?' I'd say. My eldest boy would beg the same of me only a few years later, and Freddie, my youngest son who's now six, would ask that exact question when I was still drinking.

I played football with my mates and cousins on the street as a very small boy back in Harlesden, but it was playing with my dad, just the two of us, every afternoon after school at the park that was my joy. He would coach me and give me advice, but didn't 'teach' me. No one can teach you to thread a pass through the eye of a needle, you instinctively know when it's on and how to judge the weight and timing of it. For me, it was in there all the time, perhaps just like the addictions.

Freddie comes home from training now and will play with his friends next door. They're lovely kids and they'll be doing rabonas and step-overs, as they've been shown. No one really does that in a game. I try to tell them that the most important skill of all is passing to a team-mate. You want to practise something? Just keep passing the ball to each other, but Freddie says, 'C'mon, Dad. You're not Ronaldo. Don't try to tell me how to play!' He knows I did play a long time ago, but he's too young to square-off who I am now with what I used to be.

My dad could see I had talent and would encourage me every day. It was him and my mum, up in the stands at Wembley, that I was proud for, more than me, when I got my

England call-up in 1991 and made my debut coming off the bench against Germany. For everything he'd done, taking me here, there and everywhere as a kid to play football – your parents have to sacrifice so much time and money – England was the big payback for all their hard work.

Although my dad was a massive Arsenal fan, I was Chelsea, through and through, and still am. I idolised the late Ray Wilkins and although they say never meet your heroes, you couldn't wish for a nicer, classier person. Many years later, I would tell him how much I loved him when I saw him and, God bless him, I'm glad I did even though, typical of him, he would get embarrassed and say, 'Turn it in, Merse.' But as a kid I also loved the entire league. I used to play a game when I was a kid: I'd come home from school, write all the fixtures out, throw a dice for the results and work out all the tables from the First to the Fourth Division. I would have these romantic images of the names and places, which didn't marry up much to reality when I was eighteen and on loan at Brentford and actually went to Port Vale, Darlington and Bury for the first time. I still love poring over the results pages in the Sunday papers. Those names will always have a bit of magic in them for me.

•

Football was a release from school. I was dyslexic, which wasn't properly dealt with, and also had a speech impediment, so you can imagine how I struggled. My mum says I hardly spoke at all before the age of six and she had to take me to speech therapy. Later, I had a problem saying the letter 'S' which took a few sessions to get over, but I still stumble over my words. People think I'm being lazy or thick when I mispronounce players' names on *Soccer Saturday* and have a go about it on Twitter. I've always prepared and try hard to say them properly, but sometimes the letters on the team-sheet still get jumbled up between my eyes and my brain when I reach for them. I have very neat handwriting because I really have to concentrate when doing it. I can't write quickly because I can't spell properly. I have to take my time – and write out words in the air in big letters with my index finger to practise spelling the tricky ones before I pick up the pen.

I improved at secondary school in Greenford because my PE teacher, Mr McAllister, would spend time with me working on my reading. He realised that I found books very hard and decided to try something else. Knowing my obsession with football, he started clipping the sports pages from the newspapers, which he knew would grab my attention. Another reason, I suppose, why the clubs' names really captured my imagination.

I had a knee injury in the summer before I went to Greenford High School, from sliding out of goal on the field behind our estate. Most of the houses were still being built and there was a lot of builders' junk all over the place, but we were so keen on playing football that we didn't care. A long piece of wire like a knitting needle went deep into my right knee and damaged the ligaments. Everything had to be sewn up by the surgeon, sixty stitches in total, using catgut. We were all worried about whether it was so serious that I wouldn't be able to play again, but actually in the end it made it stronger and more flexible, allowing me to use the outside of the foot as effectively as the instep, which gave me a passing range that meant I barely had to use my left, and I never had a knee problem in my career. What it did do, though, was prevent me starting high school on time. I arrived late and even then the wound on my knee became infected and started to smell. It was rank, but I didn't realise it was me and thought it was the kid I was sitting with who stank. It didn't help and, being very shy already, I was not very good at getting involved and making friends.

It was not so painful later, and being good at football was an advantage, but maintaining friendships is difficult for an addict. Sometimes, when I do an after-dinner speech there will be a table with ten lads on it and they've all known each other since school. They look as if they're in their forties and fifties, married with kids, maybe grandkids too, but they've stayed in touch. I think, 'Cor! How nice is that? I'd love that.' I haven't got that and it's a prime example of how selfish you become when addictions take over. I didn't find time to ring people or spend any proper time with my mates because my addictions completely occupied me the whole time. So you drift apart.

With other footballers it's different as you could see on *Harry's Heroes*. Perhaps it's the nature of the job – relationships can end very abruptly, you're sold, he's sold, he's your mate in the England squad for a couple of years and then he or you are never picked again. Yet you can go eleven or twelve years without seeing each other, then as soon as you meet up with all the lads, it's like it was yesterday. You've got so much shared history that the bonds run deep.

Perry Groves, my old Arsenal room-mate, was my best man at my wedding to Kate and is my best mate, but because of kids and our jobs we don't talk to each other as often as we should do. Nowadays, because of texting as well, it's changed. Instead of picking up the phone and having a conversation, you text someone to say, 'Are you okay?' You tell yourself, 'job done', but it isn't really the same.

Now I'm in recovery and doing well, I talk to people in the same situation more than my friends. If I'm struggling with wanting to drink or have a bet, I'm not ringing Perry. I need to talk to people with experience of that and you tend to hang around with people in recovery more than your mates. I won't say it's sad because I need it, but you pay a price with your other friendships. Then again, you don't want to talk about recovery all the time, every day of the week. You want a life and it's there where Perry, and my old *Soccer Saturday* colleague Phil Thompson, have given me support in different ways. Thommo has been great for me with his advice and encouragement, checking in to see how I am. You wouldn't believe how much help he's been to me just by being there.

•

I made the Brent Schools Under-11s team while still in Harlesden at the age of nine. I was a forward with decent pace and touch. I scored five on my debut against Hackney, earning a write-up in the *Evening Standard*, which is glued to the opening page of the first of several scrapbooks in my dad's collection of cuttings which he kept. They chart my life from 1977 onwards and would later include quite a few front pages as well as hundreds from the back. I was picked for Ealing Schools once we moved out west and did very well, but I was spotted when playing for my Sunday side, Forest United in Kingsbury, first by Watford followed by Arsenal, QPR, West Ham and Chelsea.

You'd think by the number of goals I was scoring, I had calmed down, conquered my nerves. The last thing you'd want in a team is an anxious striker. But inside I must have been a mess, because all the pent-up worry gave me the jitters, literally. I started having palpitations, a racing heart-beat and hyperventilating, during Sunday morning games. I used to have to ask to come off, because I thought I was about to die. Eventually, we went to the GP who looked me over and told me they were panic attacks, to focus on my breathing and they would pass. Getting used to them helped and the understanding that they would go fairly quickly stopped the fear that I was having a heart attack. I learnt to cope with them and then manage them, but they have returned at times in my life in stressful situations, only on aeroplanes recently or even at the thought of getting on one.

When I made it into the reserves at Arsenal, I rounded Peter Bonetti, Chelsea's absolute legend of a goalkeeper and one of my boyhood heroes, in one game and the panic struck again without any warning. It was right at the time when I had major doubts about making it as a professional at that level. All I had to do was tap the ball into the net, but all of a sudden I couldn't breathe. My heart was fluttering, but the rest of me froze. It gave a defender time to catch me and clear the ball. I must have looked like a right muppet and I felt really small. I went back to the doctor, who told me to pack in football if it was going to cause me so much trouble. I didn't listen to him – the pleasure outweighed the terror – and muddled through.

I started going up to Watford twice a week to train at the age of twelve and the sessions were taken by some of the first-team players. Kenny Jackett and Nigel Callaghan are the two I remember best. They were in the Second Division at the time, managed by Graham Taylor, who would give me my England debut in that Germany game and later cut me out of the picture and end my Villa career. I enjoyed going to Vicarage Road and felt comfortable around the club. I was lively on the field despite being very small and slender compared with the other lads and deep down I didn't have a huge amount of belief in myself but others would say I was naturally gifted and spoke of a bright future for me at Watford.

But Arsenal were persistent. Their scouts, Steve Burten-shaw and Bill Groves, kept watching me, came round the house a few times and stayed for hours, selling the club. They gave us tickets for a match at Highbury against Everton but none of the bungs you hear about – new washing machine for your mum or brown envelope for your dad. That wasn't the Arsenal way. Bill once stayed until 2 a.m., convincing me to sign. My dad was already sold on them but I remember running up the stairs to get away, crying my eyes out because I absolutely loved it at Watford and didn't want to go.

My dad's passion for 'the Arsenal' really swayed me when it was time to sign associated schoolboy forms at fourteen, which tied you exclusively to one club for two years. I always thought I'd have the best chance of making it at Watford, who had a family feel about them and were on the way up, rather than a bigger, established club. They all knew me there. Most of the lads at Arsenal would have been training with the club for a couple of years. Going there without knowing anyone scared me. Remember, I'd arrived late at school and never properly caught up with making friends and the thought of starting that all over again was frightening. I loved pleasing my dad, but secretly I was gutted and quite afraid.

I signed for Arsenal in April 1982, a few days before Watford were promoted and they would go on to finish runners-up in the First Division in 1983 and the FA Cup in 1984, a short-term future that was much better than Arsenal's. It wasn't just Graham Taylor from Watford to whom I will always be grateful. There's another connection. In 2019, the first person to ring me after *Harry's Heroes:*

The Full English went out and showed the moment when it all became too much with the gambling and I broke down in tears, was a lady who asked if Sir Elton John could call. I couldn't believe it but he rang me later that day and he's been in touch now and then ever since, just checking on how I am and how things are.

What a caring person he is. I know he's a massive football fan and a recovering addict himself, but he doesn't have to do that. Yet there he is, the most famous singer in the world and he puts himself out, congratulating me when I made it to a year of being sober, always encouraging. Kind words mean so much. And they can be from anyone. Truly, they all help. Last year between lockdowns, I was in Zara shopping with my wife, Kate. I was waiting with my mask on when a young lad came up to me, he was only seventeen, and said, 'I just want to say how inspiring you are. I just want to say thank you.' Wow! I thanked him back and we had a nice chat, but I am sure he wouldn't realise how much something like that means to me. I go away walking on air.

Going to Arsenal twice a week, on Monday and Thursday nights after school, was a slog. It's a long journey on the tube from Northolt but my dad came with me, to keep me company. Arsenal's 'gym' was under the Clock End but it wasn't one of those with a wooden floor, benches and wall-bars like they had at schools back then, nor was it anything like the gyms you would recognise today. It was a full-size pitch, made of shale and gravel, which would rip your trainers to shreds. It was a massive pitch when you're fourteen and it was rock hard. I hated it. I would always enjoy the journey back with my dad, who would wait for me while we were training, and we would stop off on the Holloway Road for a KFC on the way home. It was hardly the sort of diet that a fourteen-year-old academy kid would be allowed anywhere near now, but back in the day I could eat all that and stay super skinny, try as I might to add a bit of bulk.

It was my size that was holding me back. I was sharp, fast, could pass and always scored loads of goals but hadn't shot up or filled out. I still looked like a frail boy and I just wasn't being picked to play for the Under-16s on Sunday mornings. I'd be substitute, at best, maybe get 10 minutes. In the past, I couldn't get enough of football but there were days when a big, ugly centre-half would give me a kick in the first five minutes and I'd shrink. I thought I was wasting my time and by the end of two years I was convinced there wasn't a chance in hell that they would give me an apprenticeship.

I was right. They didn't. Steve Burtenshaw, the chief scout, still believed in me but I wasn't so sure about Don Howe, the manager, who was a brilliant coach and put on fantastic sessions. He had been on at me before to toughen up. When he called me into his office as I turned sixteen and was getting ready to leave school, I was expecting the worst. I knew they didn't think I was good enough and were worried about my size. Don began by telling me exactly that, confirming I hadn't earned an apprenticeship. He went on to say, though, that Arsenal had one place on the Youth Training Scheme, a Thatcher-government initiative that subsidised a year's in-work training for sixteen-year-olds in a time of mass unemployment. And that they were giving it to me. Instead of Arsenal paying me £25 a week, the taxpayer would (and receive it back a gazillion times over in income and betting tax).

It didn't bother me at all that I wasn't going down the usual path. I wouldn't have had the chance without the YTS scheme. It's hard to make it. You'll take any route you can and you have to be so lucky whichever way you go. Of course, if life gives you a break it's still down to you to take that opportunity and make a success of it. It's kind of a fitting twist that I owe the start of my career to Arsenal taking a massive punt on me. And in case I thought I was anything other than a long shot, Don said, 'If you don't get any bigger in the next year, you'll never make it as a footballer.' When he said that the first image that came into my mind was my mum and dad, who aren't giants to say the least. These days they actually do size up the parents before you're a teenager to work out whether it's worth taking you on. I felt relieved more than delighted when I left his office. That threat, or as I know he would have seen it having had to do similar things when a manager myself, an old pro's statement of a hard football truth, was hanging over me from the off. There were real doubts but I had a year to prove myself.

2

'I'M GOING INTO WILLIAM HILL. DO YOU FANCY IT?'

Arsenal were not the club or institution they had once been or would go on to become again when I joined. They finished sixth the year I turned sixteen and started on the YTS, and while they would still get crowds of up to 50,000 for Manchester United, Liverpool and especially Tottenham, they fell as low as 18,000 for some home games under Don Howe. Highbury still had the old class of the marble halls and the bust of Herbert Chapman, which the apprentices had to polish once a week. Don was a phenomenal coach, scarily ahead of his time, but not a brilliant manager. No one loved 'the Arsenal', as he always called them, more. Sadly, having stood up from being Terry Neill's number two, he found it difficult to rule the first-team squad with the iron rod that George Graham wielded so effectively later. Don would tell it to you straight – like he did when telling me bluntly if I didn't grow in a year I'd be out – but his natural personality was more good cop than bad cop.

Arsenal had won only the FA Cup in thirteen years since the 1971 Double, and despite some top signings we were a million miles behind Liverpool who dominated the league in the eighties. Discipline isn't the be-all and end-all in making a team successful and building positive team spirit. But without it, you haven't got a chance and the dressing room can split into cliques: young and old, boozers and the straights, big money buys and homegrown kids, footballers who've seen it all and those with it all in front of them, high earners and the rest. Don was old school. He valued hard work and enthusiasm as well as talent and was great with young players. But by the end in 1986, when he quit, you could sense that his frustration with some of the older ones was closer to disgust.

It was an old-fashioned football apprenticeship back then, massively different from the experience of the modern academy player at a big club today. I would have to be at Highbury by 8 a.m. so I'd get on the tube at Northolt at 6.30 a.m. every morning, using the travel card the club issued to us, and ride sixteen stops on the Central Line to Holborn, half-asleep. I'd change there for the Piccadilly Line, get off five stops later at Arsenal and head straight into the ground. Our job would be to take the skips of freshly washed training kit and load them on to the bus and then get on it ourselves for the drive to London Colney, up near St Albans. It would take about 45 minutes through the traffic at Southgate and Cockfosters and once there we would set out the kit for the first team, reserves and our lot. Then, at last, we would train under Pat Rice, the youth team coach, who was a stickler for always working flat out.

We would pick up all the dirty kit off the floor afterwards, stick it into laundry bags, put it back on the bus, have lunch, do our set of senior players' boots – how grateful you were to get a good pro who might get you a free pair from his sponsor if you did a decent job or a £50 Christmas bonus when your weekly wage was £25 – and return to Highbury to hand it all over to the kit man, Tony. It was the same routine Monday to Thursday and I would get home knackered at 6 p.m.

On Fridays we would get back to Highbury earlier and set up the ground for the match. There used to be two massive communal baths in the dressing rooms and we had to scrub them and rinse them until they were spotless and then do the individual, little baths, all the toilets and hose down all the walls and floors. Pat Rice would come round and inspect everything, running his index finger along the benches and cisterns just to make sure. We would get a bollocking if it wasn't perfect. He would make us do it all over again and stay until he was happy. At other times, we would have to sweep the snow off the North Bank, paint the crush barriers, help the groundsman and pick up litter.

We were always told, 'Remember who you are, what you are and what you represent.' This was the Arsenal way of making you feel part of something really important, really special, to have high standards. Punctuality and politeness is drummed into you. I still can't stand it if I'm late or anyone else is. The lads in the year above – David Rocastle, Niall Quinn, Tony Adams, Martin Hayes, Michael Thomas and

Martin Keown – were fantastic. The thing with Arsenal is that it's classy. It's like a private school . . . without the bullying. They recruit good footballers but they also go for good people and everyone looked out for you, kept you on your toes. That's what the club was: everybody helped everybody.

It was hard, though. We went to college one afternoon a week and I couldn't bear being back in the classroom even though Kate Hoey, who was in charge of our education and later went on to become a Labour MP, tried her best to make it interesting. I can't have learnt a thing because all I remember is that we had to work on these big, old, shitty computers and I didn't have a clue what we were supposed to be doing.

The physical part of the training was tough as well. I was quick but I don't miss those running days. One of the things we were made to do, which must have been a hangover from the twenties and thirties, was run up the North Bank terrace or from the bottom step right to the top of the Upper East Stand with one of your mates on your back. That was just a run of the mill Tuesday when we were kids and the first team had a day off. All the physiologists that clubs employ now would say, 'No way!' But that was exactly what we had to do. One of the perks of making it into the first team is that you still had to run up the stands in pre-season, but you were usually spared having to give someone a piggyback.

I didn't believe in myself at the start. Pat Rice didn't believe in me either. In my first year, I barely got a kick for the youth team. I was never picked. In one pre-season game against Manchester United's youth team, I had to run the line for the whole of the match. I was flying for once that summer and thought, 'What chance have I got here? This is absolutely ridiculous.' Most weeks, I was sub at best and quickly lost heart. Some of my mates from school were working on building sites and taking home £150 a week. I wasn't getting that a month. You can stomach £25 a week if you're playing, but I didn't even have that. I said to my mum and dad one day, 'That's it. I've had enough. I don't want to play football anymore. I just want to be with my mates.'

They went out on Fridays and Saturdays, living the life. I didn't see the long-term project – as far as I was concerned there wasn't one at Arsenal, full stop. It was so dispiriting. My dad, however, would always say, 'Stick with it.' And deep down I knew I didn't have a choice, because it's all I ever wanted. I had nothing else. I was terrible at school, I'm dyslexic, I can't talk properly. I had to be a footballer to have a good life.

I used to see a lad called Gavin Maguire, who played for QPR, at Northolt station every morning. He was seventeen and in QPR's first team, playing in the First Division, while I couldn't even get a youth team game at Arsenal. QPR, my local club, had been interested in me for years and I'd sit on the tube after he'd got off at White City full of regret, thinking, 'I should have gone to QPR and got an opportunity.' The only thing I knew how to do was carry on putting in maximum effort and hope for a break. I may have had big doubts when I was at home and disillusioned to the point of saying what I did to my parents. Who knows what I would have done had they said, 'Go on then. Pack it in.' They didn't, though, and something inside me would never give up on the bigger dream.

I just loved football. Millions do but in this instance I had the good sense to realise I was at least on the right road even if I wasn't very far along it. Making it as a professional footballer has to be one of the hardest things to achieve. If you want to be a lawyer you have to work your socks off at school, study hard for three years at college plus a couple more while you're establishing yourself in the job. You have to have dedication but it is doable. There is a path: work hard, pass your exams, do the right things and you will become a lawyer. It's the same for virtually every job in the country. Even with something in individual sports, like golf, if you've got the talent and nerve you can get there. Because it's down to you. With football, it's all about timing, opportunity, other people's opinions and, above all, luck. Everything's got to fall in your favour to make it, no matter how good you are.

Take Marcus Rashford. As an ex-player who works on telly, people in the game will tell me when they've seen a special lad. 'Cor!' they might say, 'You should see this kid at Manchester United, he's phenomenal. He'll be the best you've seen.' There was none of that buzz about Rashford at the start, but all of a sudden Anthony Martial gets injured before a Europa League game against Midtjylland, there's no other senior striker fit and Rashford at seventeen takes his chance. He never looks back. If Martial hadn't been injured, we simply don't know if he would have had the same life, do we?

Look at Jose Mourinho, one of the greatest of managers. When he was at Porto, he went to Man Utd in the Champions League last 16 and they get a free-kick in the 90th minute. They're going out on away goals. Benni McCarthy steps up to take it, shoots and the United goalie, Tim Howard, drops it. Their bloke, Costinha, taps it in and Mourinho's off up the length of the pitch, jumps on everybody, becomes this unforgettable character. They beat Man Utd, do Lyon in the quarters, a Deportivo La Coruna side whose best days were gone in the semis and get Monaco in the final. They could not have chosen better opponents. They win the European Cup and the rest is history. Yet if Howard catches that ball, as he would do ninety-nine times out of 100, does Mourinho have the career that he has had? I'm not sure. It is always about time and chance.

•

As a player, all you can do is work as hard as you can. I never missed a training session even later, after I turned pro and was drinking heavily. It didn't matter if I got in at 4 a.m. pissed, I was at work on time. I have never switched off the alarm and turned over in my life and said, 'Nah. Not today. I'm not going in.' If you do it once, you will do it again and then you have a problem.

When I got the sack from Walsall, the man who used to live in the apartment underneath me, Roy, asked me if I wanted to play for his Sunday side. I love playing football so I was up for it and turned up on the morning. Both managers were Tottenham fans and one of them had the cheek to say, 'I'm putting you down as sub.' I didn't moan because I'm really not the kind of bloke to do the big 'Don't you know who I am?' thing, and anyway someone didn't turn up so I played. This was only three weeks after I had left a League One club and there were five players in that Sunday league team who were good enough to play for me at Walsall. They had the skill, knew the game but hadn't had the dedication or made the sacrifices that you're forced to make as a pro. You have to want it so badly that you live a certain way from a young age. When you get to fourteen, fifteen, sixteen and your mates are discovering drink and going out, girls and whatever, you have to turn the other way. Friday was always the big night: the weekend starts here. I stayed in. And even though I knew I wasn't playing for the youth team, I still stayed in.

I wasn't enjoying it that first year, but there are a lot worse stories than mine. For some kids, they face the biggest setback imaginable at fourteen, fifteen or sixteen and they're told it's over. When you're getting knocked back at a young age like that, it's hard. It's bad enough when you go up to a girl at sixteen and they don't want to know you. Imagine that you've wanted to be a footballer all your life and at sixteen your whole world crumbles. How many of them go home, believe what they've been told and accept the judgment of a grown-up who has been around professional football for a long, long time? Most will think, 'I'm not going to be good enough' or 'I'll never be big enough.' You have to be special to go home and say, 'You know what? You're wrong.' People who get back up from that are inspirational.

I wasn't playing but I was still on the inside track. There was hope and that's what I say to every kid now: you've got to keep on going. Look at my year group and I was the only one who had an Arsenal career and yet I hardly played the first year. If you keep going, you will get that break and that's why it's so important. If you stay in it and don't walk away, you've always got a chance.

The only upside of not being involved in matches was that if the first team were short of bodies at training, I'd go over and make up the numbers while the youth team were working on shape and tactics for a game. It helped me because I was always better with better players. Believe me, playing in the Premier League is easier than playing in League One. It isn't 100 mph, you've got more time on the ball, the pitches are smoother and all your team-mates can really play. Similarly, playing with First Division players was easier than playing with seventeen year olds.

I was fortunate when I went over to join in because the older lads liked me. Charlie Nicholas, Viv Anderson, Graham Rix, Kenny Sansom all took a shine to me probably because, on the pitch, I was a little rogue. I couldn't tackle, I had no left foot but I had a good football brain. I was like that chess prodigy Beth in *The Queen's Gambit* on Netflix. Watching her, I thought, 'that's me' because I had that sort of vision and could work out things three, four, five moves ahead. I could always see the pass before it happened. If you watched me when I was on to receive a pass, particularly with my back to goal, you would have noticed that I was constantly moving my head, like a batsman at cricket scanning the field before each delivery. I didn't have a conscious thought that this pass was definitely going there. I would know where everyone was and had a picture of what they would do, so would make an instinctive decision based on this panoramic view depending on the angle and the weight of the ball into my feet. It was why I was usually a step ahead of the other players. I don't want to sound flash but I could see things on the pitch that other players couldn't see. I could lie in bed before a game and visualise situations in matches. I would plot exactly how it would all play out.

Some people will read this and laugh, 'You couldn't see that all your horses wouldn't win.' And they're right. I couldn't see all the addictions staring me in the face but I could see a pass out of the back of my head. It's the gift that made me as a footballer. I have wondered sometimes whether it was my illness that made me play like I did. Because my life off the pitch was a free-for-all, I never lived safely. Everything was always a drama away from football and consequently I couldn't play safe on the field either. Later, some of the lads used to pull their hair out: 'Stop trying to play the fucking glory ball all the time.' But I could see the pass and that was the only reason I played it. I wouldn't bottle it if I could see it, because it would be like cheating yourself and the team.

Being brave isn't all about steaming into 30-70 tackles. It's also about getting on the ball and trying what you see to create something for your team even when it isn't going well. I would do that even at sixteen. I was nowhere near a youth team place, but it showed the first-team lads that I was on the same wavelength as them and had the 'balls' you need to play upfront with footballers of that quality. I was fine in that company on the training field. I'm shy but the football pitch was always a comfort zone. Weirdly, the competitiveness didn't spook me, nor did their fame. I've always liked winning. I'm all right when I know what to do. Talking to people for a kid like me was hard, but once I'd learnt how to control the anxiety I could handle playing with or against them.

I was six stone wet through at the beginning of my YTS but completely out of nowhere, given the size of my parents and grandparents, as the year went on I started to shoot up. From tiny and skinny I grew to be slim and lanky, which gradually began to change Pat Rice's mind. After about seven months, he started to pick me. I was the classic late developer, coming up on the rails to overtake all the good players, who reached maturity ahead of me and had once seemed out of sight. We had lads like Wes Reid, Lawrie Osborne, Greg Allen, Roger Stanislaus, Paul Smith and Nick Hammond who would go on to play professionally but not at the level they once thought they would reach. After just over a year, they gave me a pro contract worth £150 a week. Finally, I was on building site money! From £100 a month to £600 . . . I thought I was the richest man in the world.

Gradually I began to make an impact and started at centre-forward in every round of the FA Youth Cup in 1985–86 when we got to the two-legged semi-final and lost to Manchester City on penalties. Most of those City players went on to play for the first team – Paul Lake, Paul Moulden, Steve Redmond, David White, Andy Hinchcliffe, and Ian Brightwell – while we had only me and Michael Thomas from the year above who made it. But it was a very tight couple of matches – I scored in the first leg, then had my penalty saved in the shootout before the referee ordered a retake and I put that one in.

I played in the Southern Junior Floodlit Cup as well, but it was an indoor competition, of all things, that gave me the biggest push forward in my career. The Guinness Soccer Six was a midweek tournament held in Manchester and shown on *Sportsnight*, which for years was BBC One's midweek sports programme shown late on Wednesday nights, presented by Harry Carpenter. Arsenal had to send a team but George Graham, who had become the manager in the summer of 1986, wouldn't risk most of the first-team boys because of injuries. I went up with Gus Caesar, Michael Thomas, a few from the youth team plus a couple of experienced players, Graham Rix and Tommy Caton, who had dropped out of George's plans. This was during the ban on English clubs playing in Europe after Heysel and there was hardly any football on TV. I had one of those days. Everything I tried came off and Tony Gubba, the commentator, was raving about me, going properly purple.

We were playing against older pros who didn't bust a gut. The trip was a bit of a jolly for them and they made us look better than we were. We lost in the final to Oxford United but played really well, and afterwards Charlie Nicholas did a newspaper article about me saying, 'He'll be the next Ian Rush.' Charlie was the top man back then, adored by the North Bank and knowing he would not have said it without reason gave me such incredible belief. The first-team boys were so kind to me, some, like Charlie with his generosity of spirit and open, welcoming warmth, others in a tougher way. I owe so much to the former England midfielder Steve Williams. He was fiery, hard on me relentlessly in the reserves, constantly hammering me. At first I'd think, 'Why me? Why are you picking on me all the time?' He would be shouting after every little mistake, 'What the fuck are you doing? Why are you giving the ball away, you fucking cunt?' Today, they would say he was a bully and I don't think you can do that in the game anymore. After a while, though, I began to love it. I came to appreciate that he was drumming into me what it took to make it, maintaining an urgent tempo, the importance of keeping the ball and never letting your standards drop even when you're a thirty-year-old international stuck in the 'stiffs'. The loss of reserve-team football and its replacement with Under-23 sides has, I think, harmed player development. Steve rated me and all he wanted was to make me the best player I could be, to be more selfish in front of goal, to get my bad habits out of the way and behind me.

'Look after yourself, son, and you won't go far wrong,' Steve once said when it was clear all his advice and scolding had rubbed off on me. If only bad habits elsewhere in my life were as simple to get behind me.

•

I had my first drink at about the age of fifteen. I had a couple of mates round the house one night when my mum and dad had gone out and we found a bottle of Pernod. We demolished it, and, boy, was I sick. You would think that the first time you're hideously ill, it would put you off alcohol. In fact, although it might put you off that particular drink – and Pernod and black made a hell of a mess when it came back up again – you go completely the other way. Every youngster will recognise the moment when the room spins as you put your head on the pillow for the first time and you swear you won't touch another drop. No chance of that. I loved the way it made me feel right from the start.

People at Alcoholics Anonymous speak about drink in different ways. I've heard some say, 'I loved it, loved the very taste of it.' I never did. I didn't go into a pub, take the first sip of a pint and go, like some regulars, 'Aaaaaaah! That's lovely.' I never drank because I liked it. I drank for the effect. Anxiety ate away at me. Looking back, I can't think specifically what it was that was making me like that because it wasn't one thing. I was worried about everything all the time. My head was constantly churning with thoughts and doubts. Away from football I was very quiet, my personality was buried within myself. In social situations, I wouldn't say boo to a goose. When I had a girlfriend for the first time, we knocked about together for a month but I never once plucked up the nerve to kiss her. But a couple of drinks brought me out of myself. It completely changed me. I would talk to anybody.

Drink was like boarding a rocket for me, a ticket to a different world. I could be the person who made everyone laugh. If I drank no one would ever know how I was feeling inside. By the time I was a first-team regular and we would go on tour, one of my party pieces was to run across night-clubs and slide across the dancefloor on my knees, knocking everybody flying out of the way. I would do all kinds of stupid things, just to impress people who were as pissed as I was but had more sense. When you're shy, you're insecure and when you do find friends, a worrier will do anything to stay onside. You will become someone else. 'Oh, here's Merse,' they would say, almost rubbing their hands because they knew I was game for anything. 'Fuck me, let's go.'

At sixteen and seventeen, I was still 'clever'. I drank at the right times, Saturday nights usually. Football was way more important to me. Later, I wouldn't be able to control it. I might think I'll only have a couple the night before a game but when you're an alcoholic, you're not having a couple. I remember once David Seaman was giving me a lift back home and we passed a pub. 'Come on,' he said. 'I really fancy a pint. Let's go in and have one, but only one because I've got to go home.' I refused and told him that it was utterly pointless having one pint. A total waste of time. I think I told him he must have been mad. I was twenty-two. By that time, one pint was too little and 100 was not enough. 'One drink' would turn into a disaster. At the end of my last, long spell of drinking I used to leave the pub after spending all Sunday there and make sure I brought six bottles of beer home with me. I couldn't just stop. I had to carry on until I fell asleep.

There were plenty of drugs around, too, in my mid-teens. I tried a bit of weed but it didn't make me feel right. I liked to have a laugh and that's why I drank and would later take cocaine. I didn't want to be spaced. I needed to get out of my head, not turn ever more inwards. All my addictions were not about trying to find myself. I wanted to lose myself. And nothing made me lose myself more than gambling.

I had my first bet at the age of sixteen. Four weeks into the YTS and on the last Friday of the month, Pat Rice handed out the brown envelopes with the wage slips in. I went with my mate Wes Reid from the youth team up to the Barclays in Finsbury Park where we cashed them in. I had £100 for the first time in my life. 'What are you doing now?' I asked Wes once we both had our money. 'I'm going into William Hill,' he said. 'Do you fancy it?'

Those nine words changed my life. It's still a bit of a blur what happened. Walking into the bookies, I remember, blew me away. As soon as we were through the door I was removed from the moment, in another dimension. If drinking was like getting on a rocket to zoom into another world, a means to an end, this was like being on a spaceship where you're aware of and completely absorbed in the journey.

You're insulated from all your worries. Nothing back there on Planet Normal matters now. When you're trying to make it as a footballer, you have these thoughts all the time. Will I make it? I've made it this far, but what happens next, knowing the further you go the bigger the crash if you just fall short? You have to be focused all the time and it takes a toll. The betting shop for me sparked an out of body experience. It was like a safe haven. All of a sudden, I felt I could sit in here all day.

All day.

I was skint in 10 minutes. Instead of giving my mum a few quid, I pretended I'd been mugged on the way home, scratched up my face by rubbing it on a brick wall, and subbed money off her for the next month. That night in bed, I said the unaware addict's catchphrase, 'Never again! Never again!' But as the days ticked by, I couldn't wait for payday. Not to make amends but to go into the bookies again. I loved the thrill of it. I was hooked.

3

WILD THING

George Graham is not the person you think he is.

Yes, he could be very tough and ruthless, strict about organisation and discipline on the pitch, very single-minded, stubborn and focused on winning to the point of an utter obsession. It wasn't for nothing that we called him 'the Ayatollah' or 'Gaddafi' ... behind his back, of course. He could, as he liked to say, come down on you 'like a ton of bricks'. He once dropped me for two months because I laughed when he told me to 'get moving' during a closing-down drill. He didn't confront me about it, just left me off the team sheet the following Saturday, blanked me and left me to stew. He did not once have to prove who was boss. There was never any doubt from the moment he came home to Arsenal in the summer of 1986, but he could also be kind, understanding, tirelessly patient, especially with me. He kicked me up the arse many, many times. He also put his arm around my shoulder when I needed it most and did his best to help those who loved me cope with the mess I was making of my life.

If you talk to almost everyone else about George – and I'd never dare refer to him as George, back then it was always 'Gaffer' or 'Boss' – they'd say, 'He ruled with an iron fist in an iron glove.' I was with him longer than almost anyone and in trouble more than most. I must have been in trouble almost every other week. But he never got rid of me. George was very practical – if you were valuable to him, useful to Arsenal and, crucially, you could play, he would ultimately always fight for you. I asked him once after all the trouble I'd caused why he didn't get rid of me. 'Simple,' he said. 'If you've got a Morris Minor and it breaks down, you chuck it away and get another one. If your Rolls Royce breaks down, you get it fixed.' Had he thought I couldn't play to the standard he expected, I am certain that I would have been gone. But despite everything else, he always liked me and thought I could do that.

He used threats, bollockings, fines and suspensions when my illnesses took hold and after I did some outrageous things that were splashed all over the papers, but he never gave up on me. There was always time to sit me down in the office for advice, and he threw the support of the entire club behind me and my family whenever it seemed I was in danger of being overwhelmed by my addictions. I disappointed him many times, sure, but I think it was frustration he felt at my behaviour more often than anger and his concern and affection for me never died.

Everyone was on trial as soon as George walked through the door. We all had six weeks to prove ourselves – especially, and this is what made George different, the senior players. Look at the big hitters in Don's side: Viv Anderson,

Kenny Sansom, Charlie Nicholas, Steve Williams, Paul Mariner, Tony Woodcock and Graham Rix. They were all internationals and were all gone within eighteen months. They were top players, but they loved to live the life of top players. 'Pension players,' George called them, achievers who, he said, and I thought wrongly, were now focused on their earnings. I must say Charlie and Graham were brilliant with me. I was only eighteen when they took me to String-fellows for the first time. Champagne was on tap, the place was full of models and I was gobsmacked not only by the bill. That night I crashed round Charlie's and woke up in his beautiful Highgate apartment. This was the high life.

That's the last thing George wanted for any of the young lads. He wanted us indoors at night and, ideally, married. But the main reason he got them out of the club was because he didn't want to be questioned. Experienced players have strong opinions and don't always pull in the same direction as the manager. I don't think there was any personal dislike – he just wanted youngsters who were going to listen, simple as that.

I saw it from the other side at the age of thirty-four when Graham Taylor took over from John Gregory as Aston Villa manager late on in my fourth season there. I said something I shouldn't have said at his first team meeting when he was talking about how he'd taken Watford from the Fourth Division to the First, twenty years earlier. It was ancient history to most of the boys and I thought I had to make that point before he lost the room. Jlloyd Samuel, Lee Hendrie,

Darius Vassell and Gareth Barry weren't born when Graham got Watford going and I couldn't stop myself shaking my head and laughing. 'Come on, it's 2002, Gaffer,' I said. 'It's not going to wash anymore.' I was the captain and senior pro. Rehab, especially group therapy, had made me honest, brutally so at times. Tact came along much later. I had a massive influence with the younger players there and, having said what I said, he didn't want me around the club after the season finished. I understood, though, because I'd seen it at eighteen.

It wasn't just the England and Scotland players that George chiselled out. Stewart Robson and Tommy Caton, who were much younger, were also quickly on their way. Only Dave O'Leary survived to win two League Champion-ship medals, and even he was given only a one-year contract at first to show he would play George's way.

George's way was very regimented. If you asked me on a Monday in 1989 to predict what we would be doing on a Monday in 1993, I could tell you exactly. We would be run-ning. Everything was the same week-in, week-out, so when we went out on to the pitch, every move was as natural as waking up in the morning and cleaning your teeth. It was automatic, like clockwork. If, say, Lee Dixon had the ball in one position, I had to be in a certain place. If he had it a couple of yards further forward, Alan Smith would come short and I would push on to their centre-backs. It was ingrained into us exactly what we had to do, exactly what positions we had to be in when we did and didn't have the ball. If a wide player got to the byline, for example, we'd know he would always stand a cross up to the back post. If he was forced inside, he would float it to the near post. Or if their centre-half had the ball, one of the strikers had to press and the other drop off. If both pressed and they could play through our attack onto the midfield, he'd blow his whistle and you'd have to do it again. If you did it in a game, God help you.

He worked really hard with the back four, goalkeeper and defensive midfielder and we would play a lot of 11 v 6, trying to wear them down. By the end, they were so good we'd be lucky to score one. We did possession work, shape and how to stop runners. It was always the same but done relentlessly. *Groundhog Day* had nothing on those sessions year after year. It was about building a platform to play, where patterns become instinctive. George always said even if we didn't enjoy working with him, at the end of our careers we would have our medals and realise all the hard work and harsh words had been worthwhile. He was right.

George's knowledge of football was second to none. To measure his influence, just look at his players more than thirty years on: Lee Dixon works for NBC and ITV, Steve Bould was a coach at Arsenal for twenty years, Tony Adams has been a manager in England, Azerbaijan and Spain, David O'Leary managed Leeds and Villa, Martin Keown is on the BBC and BT Sport, Nigel Winterburn does radio work, Paul Davis is a top FA coach, Perry Groves and Ray Parlour are regulars on talkSPORT, I'm on Sky, so is Alan Smith, and

Ian Wright does *Match of the Day* and ITV. There can't be any other club that has so many people from our era working in the media and coaching. It's because we learnt football, we were taught. I don't mean that George Graham taught me how to shoot and pass. But no one was ever brought in and told, 'Just go out and play.' He taught us tactics, how to set teams up, how to go to places and beat teams who were solid, how to take on teams who could play, how to pick off sides who were very good at attacking, how defenders could support attackers and when to retreat, how to shut teams down from front to back. So much thought, organisation and preparation went into everything we did.

He was a stickler, too, for the club blazer and tie. We'd go on tour pre-season, mid-season and post-season to places like Largs in Scotland and further afield to Marbella, Cyprus, Florida, Australia, Singapore and South Africa and we would always have to wear them in sweltering heat when travelling together. Wearing the uniform was his way of stressing 'Remember what you represent.' But he did once let us undo the top buttons of our shirts in 100F heat when we caught a boat out to Great Keppel Island off the coast of Queensland.

•

George got off to a flyer and we were top of the league when he gave me my debut against Manchester City in the November of his first season in charge. We were 3–0 up when I went on for Niall Quinn with 13 minutes to go. I was buzzing, but with my first touch I crossed the ball and it sailed over the bar and into the North Bank. I thought, 'Oh my God!' I didn't think I was all that good anyway, so you can imagine how low I felt. The crowd didn't groan too loudly, though, which was a relief.

The Guinness Soccer Six at the G-Mex was a fortnight later and it convinced Brentford, who had been watching me, to take me on loan in January. Frank McLintock was their manager, Arsenal's Double-winning captain from 1971 and George's best mate. They were seventeenth in Division Three. I signed on the Thursday, trained on the Friday and was sub on the Saturday against Port Vale away. We lost 4–1 and on the way home on the coach, Frank was sacked. I thought, 'Oh God, I've got a month here!' Steve Perryman, the former Tottenham captain, was playing for Frank and took over as player-manager. He was absolutely brilliant and I was there for another eight games. I loved it there. It was a proper man's league and though I didn't score a goal, I learnt so much. The players looked after me. As a big Chelsea fan it was great that I got to play with Micky Droy, one of my heroes, and Wayne Turner was an excellent captain. If anyone did something to me on the pitch, they were straight into them. Andy Sinton was also making his way in the game, out on Brentford's left wing, and five years later we'd both be in England's squad at Euro '92. You would have got majorly long odds on that at Griffin Park.

It was there that I started drinking heavily after matches. I remember playing Bolton away in midweek, which turned out to be my last game for them. We won 2–0 and as soon as the whistle went one of the lads threw his clothes straight on without having a bath and ran out of the ground to the off licence to get the beer for the way home. Every away trip was the same whether we'd played well or not. The drinking cured my shyness in front of those experienced professionals. And I could drink, that was the thing. I could easily manage twelve pints. I prided myself on it. 'I'm not one of them nauses,' I'd think. 'Drink two pints and that's it.' I was one of the lads. It was like I'd found the only thing other than football I was good at. So, of course, I carried on doing it.

Steve Perryman saw straightaway that I had a problem at that early age. I was eighteen, on the bus and in the bar with all the older lads, putting pint after pint away, the quiet one turning louder and lairier with each drink. It wasn't so much the amount but the way I was drinking, almost inhaling it like I couldn't get enough. There was something enjoyable back then about the sensation of having a large volume of liquid gushing down my throat. Steve knew but thought, 'He isn't my player, why fix something that isn't bust? If he performs on a Saturday, leave him to it.'

That's how all managers saw it until fairly recently. And to be fair, as long as you were doing your job you would think they had no right to have a go at whatever you got up to in the rest of your life, so long as it was legal. I've seen Steve quite often since and he has said to me, 'The number of times I wanted to say something to you. But what was the point?' He's right, I wouldn't have listened. Not at eighteen. Not at forty-eight. You can't successfully stop when someone else wants you to stop. You have to get to the point where you accept, of your own free will and without being forced, that you've had enough and you want to change. You can't be doing it for the FA, for your manager, club, teammates, not even for your parents, wife and kids. You have to want to do it for yourself, when you reach the end and are fed up of being fed up. It would take me half a lifetime to understand that.

Brentford was the making of me as a footballer. I played seven league games for them when I was eighteen and yet for thirty-five years I've always looked out for their results, every game without fail. Steve wanted me to stay for the rest of the season and I was happy to commit to that. Playing first-team football in the Third Division was far more meaningful than reserve football in the London Combination with Arsenal, but I was recalled from the loan deal by George after six weeks and I knew they wouldn't have bothered doing that unless I had a chance of playing. Arsenal had been top of the league when I left despite George telling the press all season that we weren't ready. Four winless games plus Perry Groves and Charlie Nicholas being injured dragged me back. I got about half an hour at Stamford Bridge in a 1–0 defeat and that was me done for seven games, back to the reserves. Niall Quinn got injured shortly after Arsenal won the League Cup and I played five of the last six games, just after my nineteenth birthday.

My full debut, in the No 9 shirt, was against Wimbledon at Plough Lane and I scored the first with a header in a 2–1 win. Luck played some part again because Lawrie Sanchez tried to clear it off the line with his hand but thankfully only punched it in. If he had managed to tip it over, I wouldn't have scored because I wasn't on penalties. Two days later on Easter Monday we played Leicester, whose centre-forward, Alan Smith, we had signed but had let him stay there until the end of the season to help with their relegation fight. One of the morning papers had written 'Merson shows the magical touch' and 'the only mystery about this match was why Arsenal paid £800,000 for Alan Smith when they have such a promising youngster as Paul Merson in reserve.' I played well again in our 4–1 victory but they got their answer about Alan in the next match and across the following eight seasons.

We went to Maine Road to play Man City, my third start on the bounce. Everything had gone so well I thought I was 'the big I am' and 'this is a doddle'. City were going down and I was full of confidence. We kicked off, I ran up front and Mick McCarthy smashed me right in the mouth with his forearm and said, 'You fucking come near me again and I'll snap you in two.' And I thought, 'You know what? That'll do me.' I never went near him again. I couldn't wait to get off. I was petrified. I thought, 'My God, this isn't for me.' I was relieved to be substituted and George dropped me for the next game. It was only as I got older that all the physical stuff wouldn't bother me. I was back in for the last two games and scored at Loftus Road, which was virtually where I was brought up. It was always my favourite ground to play at. Boxing Day 1982 for me was QPR v Chelsea and I've loved it ever since. It's tight, whoever you play for it's full – Chelsea used to take seven or eight thousand fans. Arsenal would take six or seven thousand but even when I played for Middlesbrough, the away end would be rammed. I scored in the last game of the season, as well, three in five games and thought, 'Here we go.'

•

I went on an England Under-19 tour of Brazil and Uruguay that summer with Don Howe as coach. It was a real big deal at that age to go to Rio and Montevideo and places like that, phenomenal. It should have been a great trip to be on, but I was homesick. I had a volatile relationship with my girlfriend at the time, Lorraine. We'd bought a house in St Albans not long after I turned pro at seventeen and most of what I remember about going to South America is thinking about the relationship, our on-off engagement, wedding plans and what I was going to do. I was already drinking loads and would be banned for drink-driving when I got back to the UK. What happened was, I had been on a long session and decided to drive my new car home from the pub. Dinging a couple of other cars as I reversed out didn't concern or delay me. It was only when I missed the turning for my house because I was going too fast and wrapped the car round a lamp-post that I realised how pissed I was. I climbed out, noticed that the top half of the lamp-post was now in my neighbour's garden and panicked. I legged it back to the pub and sat down with my mates as if nothing had happened. My plan was to make out the car had been nicked. So when the police inevitably arrived soon afterwards and told me the whereabouts of my car, I played dumb. 'You're joking me?' I said. When the officer asked if I was saying it had been stolen, I replied, 'Yeah, it must have been because I haven't moved all night.' He seemed to believe me but just as I thought I'd got away with it, an older lady sitting at another table shouted across, 'He's only just come back. I saw him leave earlier in his car.' I was breathalysed, arrested and taken to the police station, three times over the limit. The copper who collared me did say that I wasn't the worst offender that night, which was the only straw I could clutch. They had just nicked someone six times over driving a JCB through St Albans town centre. I was banned for eighteen months. Not that it gave me a moment's pause for thought, even though Arsenal fined and suspended me as well. I wasn't embarrassed about it, though I knew it was serious. I laughed it off as all part of my growing reputation as a bad boy, a delusion that would screw with my head when pissed over the next few years, and screw it so badly at my worst that I used to fantasise about walking onto the pitch to 'Wild Thing'.

Our new house was between two pubs, perfect when you can't drive, I thought. I would go to both, come home at 4 a.m. paralytic, bringing some of those who'd been at the lock-ins with me. Cruelty comes easy to addicts. If you can't stand yourself, think you're an awful person, it's like a knee-jerk thing to project all that insecurity and loathing on to the people you love. That would be me – loud, argumentative and provocative to my girlfriend when she quite understandably protested about the state I was in, the lies I'd told about when I was coming home and the strangers in the living room in the middle of the night. I drank for many reasons: to stop the panic attacks, to help me overcome shyness and to keep the adrenaline rush going as long as I could after the high of a match. Basically, having always wanted to be someone else, I used drink from my mid-teens to turn me into someone else without being too bothered that by the end of the night the person I became a lot of the time wasn't very nice. For me in those days, the positives always outweighed the negatives. Not that I'd have ever thought of it as a balance sheet. Being a bit of an arsehole at home was more something I could always shrug off and justify to myself with the excuse, 'Well, I was pissed.'

I drank during the 48 hours before a game a couple of times in my career, once at Luton on Boxing Day when I just couldn't help myself boozing on Christmas Day, once a few years later when I'd been told I wasn't playing against Wimbledon on New Year's Day. George named me as a substitute to teach me a lesson and he threw me on, enraged by me nodding off on the bench. The other time was against Coventry on the opening day of the 1993–94 season when I proved to myself I'd been right when I refused David Seaman's invitation to have 'just one pint'. I'd been in the bookies with a mate after training and said I wouldn't join him for a drink over the road. 'One won't kill you,' he said. What he meant, what they all really mean, is 'one won't kill me'. If you're normal, it won't. For an alcoholic, even if I didn't recognise that I was addicted back then, one can lead to the one that kills you. Because you can't stop at one. We can drink. We can steer clear. What we can't do is drink 'responsibly'. But I got sucked into the myth of being 'Good old Merse'. I didn't want to seem like a wimp and allowed myself to be persuaded. I crawled off home at 5 a.m., got subbed at half-time the next day and was given the hair-dryer treatment by George. He dropped me for the next match as well.

Those three mistakes aside, I managed to stay dry for 48 hours before a game throughout the eight years before I went into rehab in December 1994. Yet I considered all other times fair game for a drink: Saturday nights, all day Sunday, all day Tuesday if there was no midweek game and Wednesday night if you could face it after the night before. If we did play on a Tuesday or Wednesday, we would just drink after the match, which was made easier on away trips by me importing that custom from Brentford and grabbing a couple of crates of lager, not from an off licence but the players' lounge, for the journey home. I didn't drink in fancy places. I wasn't really a wine bar or club man. There are no pictures of me with big bottles of champagne or Del Boy cocktails with sparklers coming out of them. I drank with the fans. I was never 'big time' and never forgot where

I came from. I'd drink in an Irish pub near to Highbury, the Bank of Friendship, or the Alwyn Castle and would end up in places you'd never enter sober on the Holloway Road, Islington, Kings Cross or further out at Apex Corner. This was before the licensing laws had been relaxed and London was full of gambling dens, after-hours members' clubs, dodgy pool halls, the kind of places people would look at you and go, 'What the fuck's he doing in here?' I got a kick out of being in those places, they suited the image I had of myself – a proper geezer, a legend, Jack the Lad.

While my drinking was already top-flight material by the following season, I was in and out of the side, exiled for giggling at George on the training field, and then on the bench a lot. He put me on a weights programme to develop upper body strength and it took until the spring for me to get a run of starts. The second season as a first-team player hadn't panned out like I'd hoped and as he began to get the team he wanted together, despite me scoring two against Charlton and Sheffield Wednesday and working well with Alan Smith, I feared I'd be out. More famous names than me had already left.

Footballers can't afford to be sentimental about their team-mates because when they're sold they tend to vanish in the night. Still, I was sad to see Charlie, Rixy, Kenny Sansom and Steve Williams go. This was where George really showed his genius. He had a plan to play a certain way and looked for players who had ambition, character, spirit and would, like those of us who'd come up through the ranks, owe him for giving them the opportunity. He made us into a great team but it didn't start that way. He got players from everywhere – Lee Dixon and Steve Bould from Stoke, Alan Smith from Leicester, Nigel Winterburn from Wimbledon, Brian Marwood from Sheffield Wednesday and Kevin Richardson from Watford. These weren't fashionable or successful clubs and he didn't pay high prices. Jurgen Klopp is exactly like that, bringing in footballers with real drive from Hull City, Southampton, Newcastle, Stoke, Roma and the like. Both had a structure, both wanted players with a burning hunger to achieve something in the game. It was all coming together nicely at Arsenal. I just didn't know if I would be part of it.

4

THE TUESDAY CLUB

Kerry Dixon, Tony Cottee, Frank McAvennie. Any one of them could have stopped me from playing in a title-winning side at the age of twenty-one. Any one of them could have made me miss out on the ecstasy of Anfield '89 and their names could now be permanently identified with the most dramatic night in English football history. For a whole year, Arsenal were linked with strikers and even had bids accepted for Cottee and McAvennie. According to the papers, Cottee was being bought all the way through the summer of 1988, McAvennie for most of the following spring. Both of them were top forwards who scored bundles of goals. In those days if you were bought for money, you played. Had they signed, I wouldn't have been in the team. Managers lived and died by their signings. It could cost them their job if they failed.

Cottee chose to go to Everton, McAvennie back to West Ham from Celtic. Arsenal were willing to pay the fees but were not prepared to pay them the £2,000 a week they could get elsewhere. Until fairly recently, as I found out myself in 1996, Arsenal were always reluctant to pay big wages compared with their rivals. The club never really 'looked after' its players in that way in those days. Playing for 'the Arsenal' was supposed to be more important than mere money and it also worked in George's favour to keep us 'hungry'.

It worked in mine, too, that summer. When Cottee eventually turned us down, Arsenal were stuck with me, who had started 13 games in two years, and Alan Smith, who had been called a flop for scoring only 11 goals in his first season. The rest is history. Smudger won the Golden Boot and I was Young Player of the Year. My award was the best thing you could win at my age and it was special because it was voted for by all the players in the league. I was going to pick up the award in April but the day before the Hillsborough Disaster happened, which made it feel utterly meaningless. I didn't want it anymore. It was so, so sad what happened. Football went out of the window for me at that moment, like it did for every fan, every person.

Winning the league was typical Arsenal in the way that we did it. We worked hard, we trained hard, we drank hard and we won. We were a really good team. Solid. We weren't all great mates, far from it. We'd never mingle with our wives and all that kind of thing. A couple of them might – Alan Smith and Steve Bould did – but you wouldn't get all the lads out together with their wives at once. Never.

It would probably have been better for me if we had because I would still drink with my old mates, fans, even strangers to whom I'd given out my home telephone number when paralytic and full of boozy friendliness. It allowed me to keep everything separated, so no one ever had a proper handle on how much and how often I was drinking. You become a massive liar when you're an addict. But there's another kind of dishonesty, too. Secrets can be just as harmful as lies when hiding stuff means you don't even have to come up with crap, fake excuses. I worked hard to make sure no one had the full picture. That's why when I went public about the cocaine, alcoholism and compulsive gambling, so many people who thought they knew me were shocked. None more so than my team-mates, who might see me pissed on a Tuesday or pissed off that a big bet had gone down but had no idea by the end that my life was like that virtually 24/7.

Although we didn't socialise together, we all respected each other like mad. In that Arsenal team, everyone looked after everybody else. We all worked our socks off. Everybody knew their job. It's a rare thing, you realise later in your career, to be in a team where everybody is pulling in the same direction, with such camaraderie. You take it for granted when you're in a team like that, but it's revealing that I never won a thing without those lads beside me. I've got five medals from eight years as a first-team regular at Arsenal and nothing from the nine years afterwards. No, I didn't want to go to a restaurant with them on a Saturday night, but on a Saturday afternoon at 3 o'clock I wouldn't want to be with anybody else.

Take David Rocastle. Now there was a man. I always say I've never heard a bad word said about David, and that includes before he died so heartbreakingly young. It's the biggest compliment you can give anyone in professional football, because in the game people gossip and talk behind each other's backs all the time. He was the ultimate winger and I still haven't seen one quite like him today. He was doing step-overs, the kind Cristiano Ronaldo does, thirty-odd years ago. I think he was the hardest winger who ever played in the modern era. David would steam into 40–60 tackles, absolutely steam in. He wasn't scared of anybody. No winger, believe me I played enough out there, wants to get kicked but he wouldn't flinch. He could score goals – I've seen him chip the goalie at Anfield, lob the keeper at Aston Villa and catch Peter Schmeichel off his line from 30 yards at Old Trafford. I couldn't speak more highly of anyone. He was Arsenal through and through. Loved the club. I've never seen anyone so devastated at leaving a club. Everything about him – his confidence, manner, his kindness and reliability made him the prime example of the person I wished I could be. David was such a nice man and a proper footballer. I can't believe he's gone. Even after all these years I find it so, so sad and get choked up just talking about him.

I scored 10 goals in our first title-winning season but if you look at the video of all the other 63 Arsenal goals in 38 games, if I'm still on the pitch I'm jumping all over the goalscorer. In December 1987, I'd signed a new contract on £300 a week and was pleased to do so, it doubled my money. That seemed mega. I was on £15k a year basic at twenty-one when I became Young Player of the Year and we won the league. But I was on a £525 win bonus. So I could almost triple my wages every time we won a match. No wonder I was first to every celebration! I'm all over those pictures. I'm a great believer in incentives like that. It keeps you hungry. Now kids in the Young Player of the Year bracket and loads of Premier League youngsters nowhere near a starting place can be on anything up to £60k a week. It's not their fault because clubs are in the position where if they don't do that, they're going to lose a player. If they don't pay, someone else will. For the player, I imagine it's hard to improve your game if you're on that sort of money at first. You would think, 'I'm doing well, doing my job or otherwise I wouldn't be getting this amount of money a week.' If the market says they should be on £30k a week, it should be split into £10k a week basic, £10k if you're in the matchday squad and £10k if you win the game. There's your £30k. If you don't want to work hard and perform and get in the first team, you're not worth £30k a week.

It's hard to find people with any sympathy for such high earners at such a young age. But I feel for them, I really do. You're getting so much money straightaway but football isn't about straightaway. The career has to be about longevity. Earning £30k a week from seventeen to twenty is not going to do you any long-term favours. You might 'live the dream' for three years, but what are you going to do for the next sixty-five if it doesn't work out and your next move is to League One on £800 a week? Agents have such an important role in helping them invest their money. It goes so quickly. Careers are brutally short and the chances of youth team stars maintaining it at that level are slim. They earn great money but the comedown from a £30k-a-week lifestyle at twenty to a £40k-a-year life at twenty-one can destroy people. They'll have their memories, of course, and memories are great. But they're no substitute for proper advice and planning.

Eddie Howe asked me to go down to Bournemouth a couple of years ago to talk to the players about everything, about life, about me. I remember sitting there and saying that with the amount of money they were earning, they should already be asking themselves serious questions about the future. The only ways they should ever need to work again for financial reasons are either a horrible business venture goes wrong or their accountant's a crook or they have a string of messy divorces. They should be able to save and invest enough so they are never forced to work again. Naturally, they will want to work again but it's about necessity, not needing to do it to feed your family. Work to occupy yourself rather than to eat. No one really wants to finish and play golf for the rest of their lives even if it sounds appealing at thirty-five. Everyone, eventually, wants a purpose. What are you going to do with your time otherwise? Sit indoors and do nothing? My wife Kate is a schoolteacher and she still works two days a week despite us having three young children, because she loves it and it keeps her brain going. Everybody needs something to do or it's going to be like lockdown for the rest of your life. Imagine how soul-destroying that would be.

•

Norwich were the pace-setters in 1988–89 but we caught them in December and the New Year during a run in which I scored five in six. By the end of February, we were 19 points clear of Liverpool which was unheard of – they had dominated football for as long as I could remember and had won every trophy going. It was almost drummed into us: finish above Liverpool and you win the league, simple as that. For years they brushed teams aside. They started the season at evens to win the title, which shows you how good they were but, even though they had four games in hand, 19 points is massive. They went on a ridiculous winning run after losing on New Year's Day and we wobbled a bit with three draws and a defeat at Nottingham Forest in five games. Our match against them was postponed following Hillsborough and football was shut down for two weeks to mourn the victims. When we started playing again, our lead was down to three points and they had a game in hand. It was neck and neck and after we had lost to Derby at home and drawn with Wimbledon, they moved three points ahead of us with a 5–1 victory over West Ham with only the match between us to play. Leroy Rosenior is the forgotten hero of all this – had he not scored for West Ham against Liverpool we would have had to go to Anfield, where we hadn't won for fifteen years, and win by three goals, not two, on the Friday night.

If you were old enough in 1989, it doesn't matter whether you were in Halifax or Cornwall or who you support, you remember that game and what you were doing. It was a JFK moment for football fans. The drama of it looms so large in English football history that we made a film about it. It was the biggest league game there's ever been, the two top teams after the season has finished for everyone else, going head-to-head for the title, on a Friday night at a time when hardly any games were shown live on the telly. It was the most important game Arsenal had played for eighteen years and George judged it perfectly.

We went up on the morning of the game. To Liverpool! A 200-mile coach ride on the morning of the most significant match of our careers. There was method to what seemed like the manager's madness. He didn't want us hanging around in Liverpool overnight, letting the nerves kick in early or allowing the locals to wind up the tension. Graeme Souness wrote a piece in the *Daily Mirror* that morning with the headline: 'Arsenal do not have a prayer.' Rocky read it out on the coach and someone shouted out, 'Let us pray!' It might have been me! But realistically I didn't think we could win. No way. Liverpool had much better players than us and were in unbelievable form. We'd lost to Derby . . .

After the players had had a kip – not me, I could never manage the afternoon nap, I'd watch the TV and stick some bets on – we had tea and toast and George made his famous speech, setting up what would happen to a tee. 'Keep it tight,' he said. 'Don't go mad trying to score two goals in the first 15 minutes. If Liverpool score first tonight the game's over, you'll have to get three goals and you'll never do that at Anfield.' He was bang on there – as the papers kept reminding us, they hadn't lost by two goals at home for more than three years. 'So keep it really tight, first half. Pressure, pressure, pressure all over the pitch. It's okay if it's 0–0 at half-time. You'll go out for the second half and score in the first 15 minutes and then, last 15 minutes, I'll change the shape, they'll bottle it and you'll score late on.'

I turned to Steve Bould and said, 'What's he on?' We ran out onto the field with bouquets of flowers to commemorate the people who had died at Hillsborough. As I came out of the tunnel, I looked left and our section was half empty. 'Oh my God!' I thought. 'Even our fans don't believe in us.' But there had been a big traffic jam on the motorway and all of a sudden, it filled up.

I barely got a kick in the first half. They had a lot of the ball, but we did exactly as George said and it caught Liverpool by surprise. It's a funny one, knowing you can lose 1–0 and still win the main prize. That, and the fact that we didn't have a right go at them, didn't go all gung-ho, shocked them and they weren't the Liverpool we expected and had come to fear. We worked hard, kept our shape and George was absolutely made up at half-time. 'Brilliant,' he said. 'The plan's working perfectly.'

Alan Smith put us 1–0 up eight minutes into the second half. Liverpool tried to twist the referee's arm that Alan hadn't touched what was an indirect free-kick but he had

. . . with his nose. Despite their protests and the din from a bellowing Kop in his ears, he stood firm. From then on, it all unfolded as George had predicted. Mickey Thomas went one-on-one with Bruce Grobbelaar . . . and hit it straight at him. That was it, that was our chance, a sitter and he'd missed. With about 15 minutes to go, George changed our shape, up went the No 11 board and I was off. It wasn't really the kind of game to suit me, it was more about putting in a shift than having the opportunity to get on the ball and play, but at least I'd contributed by working hard and playing to the plan.

I sat in the dugout, tracksuit top on, and watched it all unfold until the dying seconds. We'd had a good go, done ourselves proud but hadn't quite got there. We would have been gutted but would also know we hadn't let anyone down. And then 90 seconds into injury time, Kevin Richardson nicked the ball off John Barnes in our box. I'll never know why Barnes didn't just go and sit on it in the corner. Kev passed it back to John Lukic who threw it to Lee Dixon, which was the last thing Lee wanted. He clipped it up to Alan who turned it round the corner to Mickey, who got a fortunate deflection and raced through one-on-one with Grobbelaar. This time, though, when it was all up for grabs, he only went and did it. Think of all that pressure and the three seconds to think as he pelted through. Time can be the last thing you want at moments like that. You want instinct to kick in. Mickey was exactly the right man in the right place, though. Nerves of steel, he would never panic. And he waited and waited for Bruce to commit. When he finally did, at the last possible moment before being tackled, he dinked it over him. Watching it was like it was in slow-motion. As soon as it went in, it all speeded up again and everything went mad. The drama and occasion overshadow how great the goal was. Technically, it was one of the best I've ever seen.

Half a minute after Liverpool kicked off again, we were league champions.

I jumped all over Steve Bould and that set the tone for the rest of the night and the next four days. The Liverpool fans were good as gold and clapped us off. I remember Perry Groves saying to Bouldie and me, pointing at George, 'Look at golden bollocks. Everything he said would happen, did happen.' There was champagne in the dressing room, beers on the bus and we rocked up at a club in Southgate at 2.30 a.m. I know I was at a barbecue at Alan Smith's house on the Saturday night, the open-top bus tour and civic reception at Islington Town Hall on the Sunday and that I got home on Tuesday morning. Other than that, it's all a blur. I was a league champion at twenty-one and flying off the rails.

•

I was on the front pages for three incidents in the months after we won the title: for a brawl in a pub near my house, the drink-driving ban and for being drunk, loud and involved in a fight at the official dinner to celebrate the league championship. I became 'Soccer bad boy Merson' to the tabloids and there was part of me that didn't mind that reputation despite hating all the attention.

My drinking had become serious now. If I'd been diagnosed as an alcoholic, I wouldn't have believed it. Alcoholics were old men on park benches, red faces, beer for breakfast, knocking back wine and cider all day and night. That wasn't me. If I'd considered myself anything more than a normal lad who liked a real good drink on a night out, I'd have gone for 'binge drinker'. I know now that alcoholism isn't being on it all the time, needing it all the time. I thought, like most people still do, that alcoholics wake up with a bottle of vodka on the bedside table and need a swig to get their head straight. There are more binge drinkers in AA, I'd say, than people who drink heavily every day, who need it in their blood all the time. It's never been about a physical addiction. It's a psychological addiction for me. It's about not being able to handle one drink without it spiralling out of control. When I was on it, I was *on* it. It was always easier for me not to start than to stop when I had started. Good intentions go out of the window. Would I have wanted to drown out Norman Collier, the comedian at that Grosvenor House Hotel dinner, before I'd had a drink and embarrass the directors and manager? Of course not. But once smashed, I was a liability. I thought I was funnier than the professional comedian and the more the people I was with egged me on, the more hilarious I thought I was. I realise now they were laughing at my bad manners rather than the quality of my gags, heckles and insults. 'The Arsenal way' was all about good taste and manners. Once I'd had one drink, though, all I cared about was the next one and the more I drank the more outrageous I became. I'd kick the arse out of the night, long after it was enjoyable, until I collapsed into bed. That was me.

In my later drinking days, I'd be in restaurants with Kate and look over as the couples next to us got up at the end of their meal and sometimes they had left half a bottle of red wine. It amazed me every time. They could have been aliens to me because I could never do that. I had to finish it. Similarly, I've never been on a pub crawl. I could never see the point. It takes up too much drinking time walking from one pub to the next. Even if the first pub we went into was horrible, I'd think I might as well stay here. Wherever I laid my hat, I was in for the night.

I was in major trouble over those incidents. My wages had gone up to a grand a week so I was getting fined thousands of pounds now and after the dinner, George kicked me out for two weeks. He hauled me into his office. I said, 'The papers are always after me, they've got it in for me.' He replied, 'Sit in and watch the telly and they won't print anything.' I didn't catch on to that. I didn't understand that it was all down to me and no one else, that if you do the right things you're not going to face front-page tabloid stories about you. He suspended me for two weeks from everything, no training, nothing. But it didn't help because I sat at home drinking for two weeks. It's a vicious circle. I was scared the boozing and my behaviour would ruin my career so I drank to put my head right, to steady the anxiety.

I know now that I can't sit around doing nothing, because that's when I was at my most vulnerable, most likely to have a bet or a drink. I'm better now but the older I get the more I realise you don't need to be sitting around doing nothing. There's always something to do.

The other piece of advice George gave to me at that meeting when he banned me for a fortnight was: 'Get your priorities right, Merse. You have got to look after yourself. This will go.' I sat there nodding but I was thinking, 'Come on, George. I'm fucking twenty-one. I've got another ten, eleven years of this. At least.' He was right, though. Bang! And it's gone as quick as anything. It's weird how my mind works but on a quiet night I might be watching telly and think, I'm fifty-three now. We won the league in '89. That's thirty-two years ago. What have I done in the last thirty-two years? That's maybe how long I've got left on this planet. I think, I hope that doesn't go as quickly as the last thirty-two have. Isn't that depressing? When I was manager of Walsall, I found myself saying the same things to some of the young lads that George said to me, 'Look after yourself, this goes quick.' And I could see them thinking, 'Fuck off, Gaffer. I'm only twenty.' It was exactly how I used to be. If only you could put a fifty-year-old head on a twenty-year-old body. Still, we all learn by our mistakes, don't we? It just took me a long time.

•

I met Niall Quinn when we played together in Arsenal trials and we were as thick as thieves from the day we started in the youth set-up, in pubs, drinking clubs, snooker halls, dog tracks, racecourses and bookies: scheming, plotting, dreaming of how to win big. Horses and dogs were largely all there was to bet on back then. When I started to make it as a footballer, my dream was to do what Michael Owen is doing: buy a yard, train horses. I was into it massively. I knew every horse, yard and jockey. I studied it and knew everything about it, except how to win because I was a compulsive gambler. I bet on everything and anything that moved, running up huge debts. I borrowed money off everyone to stick on Steve Davis to beat Joe Johnson in the World Snooker Championship final. Joe Johnson was a pub singer, Steve Davis a raging certainty at seven to two on. Free money. The pub singer won. I was paying that back for months. I'd be in the betting shops all day, in my own world. In the end, I couldn't stand the places. I would carry on betting for years and years without going in them, I think, because of all the bad memories from when I was younger, associating them with everything I'd lost even though I carried on losing millions on the phone and computer.

I would drink with Niall a lot and also, later, with the Tuesday Club, whose regulars were Tony Adams, Steve Bould, Nigel Winterburn, Kevin Richardson and Perry Groves. Training on Tuesdays was always at Highbury and we would go out afterwards near the ground and end up in all sorts of places by silly o'clock. That session was always fast and wild. We were the 12-minute men, lining up the bar staff to serve us at five-pints-an-hour pace at the start until someone spewed and then we'd pull it back to every 15 minutes. Reports from his network of 'spies' would get back to George about what we'd been up to and sometimes he'd even receive letters from the public from people who'd seen me pissed in some pub or other and thought he should know. I would be called in for the same old lecture, but he stood by me.

I always had more of a licence than the others and definitely more of a long rein on the pitch. He didn't expect me to win 50-50 tackles or 40-60 ones. My job was to create and score goals. I wasn't going to stay in the team by winning tackles, I was going to stay in the team by setting up chances. I had to close down and work hard, of course. I've had fans boo me when I haven't steamed in but I knew my limitations. If fans got the hump because I wasn't winning a 50-50, I could swallow that, as George did as long as I did my job. His attitude towards me was why the lads called me 'son of', as in 'son of George'. We once played Argentina's Independiente in Miami in an end of season exhibition game and at training the day before I had an itch. So I scratched my cods. George was watching me and came over. 'Merse, are you all right? Is it your groin?' he said. I said that I was fine but he replied, 'No, sit down. Go and have a rest.' Had it been anybody else, absolutely no chance. He always liked me.

Off the pitch, while he didn't interfere in your personal life, if you crossed the line while on club duty, out came the old iron rod. We didn't kick on in the season after we won the title. We lost 12 games, six more than the year before and finished fourth. It took me some time to win back a starting place after that suspension and I was out for a month injured. I was injured as well for the last game of the season at Norwich but travelled up on the Friday morning. We found a tennis club after training and a few of us, Perry Groves, Kevin Richardson, Nigel Winterburn and me, had a couple of pints in the May evening sunshine. Later, some of the other lads joined us for one and left and then George and his staff wandered by, clocking the tables that hadn't been cleared and, no doubt, counting all the empty bottles and glasses, dividing them by five and jumping to the conclusion we'd had double or triple the three we'd actually sunk. 'Having a good time, chaps? It's always the same old faces,' he said with a smile. No bollocking at all. We'd got away scot free.

After the 2–2 draw we flew to the Far East for our usual post-season tour, playing Liverpool and South Korea in Singapore in the first week before going on to Bali for a week's holiday. We got into a few scrapes on nights out there, too, but were buzzing, sitting with our bags packed in the foyer of the hotel on the morning of our flight to Bali when the 'Norwich four' were handed our passports. We were sent home for boozing in the tennis club, 'a serious breach of club discipline', and watched the other lads board the bus for their jolly, pulling faces and taking the piss. We were so shocked, we sat in silence and didn't touch a drop on the 14-hour flight. George dragged us all into the office when he flew back from Bali and fined us two weeks' wages. He never missed a trick when it served him not to miss it. It was a costly season all-round.

5

FEAR AND LOATHING

Not one Arsenal player made it into England's squad for Italia '90. Tony Adams, Alan Smith and David Rocastle were all cut from the training squad in the weeks before the tournament and, though there had been plenty of talk about me being promoted from the Under-21s, I didn't make it either. Instead that summer, I got married at the age of twenty-two to Lorraine. Football should have been the farthest thing from my mind on my wedding night, but I spent it in a foul mood because, as usual, I'd placed a large bet on one of the day's World Cup matches. I did show some sensitivity for the occasion by switching to vodka from lager before the ceremony so I wouldn't be nipping to the toilet all day. It just seemed normal to me to have half a dozen large ones and stick a big bet on before church, because that's what I would have done on any other summer Saturday. The drinking stopped when I needed to be fit to do my job. The gambling stopped for nothing.

If you're not an alcoholic and compulsive gambler, your logic would be: it's my wedding day, let me do everything I can to make sure this is the best day possible for everyone

73

but especially me and the person I'm marrying, so we can treasure this day and all the good memories for the rest of our lives. But me, the alcoholic and compulsive gambler, I thought, 'I need a lot of drink to turn me into the person everyone likes, the life and soul, and if I back Scotland to beat Costa Rica, this wedding will cost me nothing.' If Scotland had won, my wedding would have been free, that was always my thinking. This may sound ridiculous but I was always a 'realistic' punter. I was never one of those gamblers who would bang everything on a 20–1 shot. I was always after easy money, backing the favourite, the odds-on chance that bookies hate. So I put a stake on that came to several grand, more than double the cost of the day. That's how the gambler thinks: 'It's either double the bubble or it's free.' When Scotland lost 1–0 to one of the worst teams you'll ever see at a World Cup, instead of a freebie I ended up with probably the costliest wedding of 1990.

Gutted, skint, pissed, I was sitting on the end of the bed on my own wedding night, thinking, 'I'm the biggest c--- in the world.' At moments like that the depression sinks in, your self-worth is on the floor and you think how horrible you are as a person. It's overwhelming that level of self-hatred. Everything started to snowball. The more I gambled the more I drank to soften the blow of how much I'd lost. That's how it was constantly. I'd think, 'I've lost all this money and I can't sit and think about that so let's drink even more.' It was a mad cocktail and within a couple of years it got to the stage where I couldn't physically drink enough to soften the blow, so I turned to something even stronger.

Now, I know that I just wasn't well. I thought I was a bad man who desperately wanted to become a good man and kept beating myself up for falling short. But I was an ill person who needed to get well. Not knowing the difference cost me so much time, so much destructive self-loathing that you end up feeling not quite human at all, like a shell of a man.

The weird thing about this almost lifelong desire for easy money was that I've always enjoyed working. I love playing football, watching it and talking about it. I never missed a day's training, no matter what time I got in the night before, and I'm never happier now than when I've got a full diary with Sky, working on *Soccer Saturday* and all the midweek games, too. The end goal with gambling was not to stop working. There was no end goal as such . . . just to keep betting. I used to think about winning the pools and how much I'd hate it. You'd have everything. You're chasing a dream really. If you won the lottery you've won what you're gambling for, the boat and the house, but then when you win the lottery, not that I've ever played it, there would be no point to gambling anymore and certainly no fun in it.

That just sums up the illness. I've never bought a ticket for the lottery because I can't even win on a 1–5 shot, so I've got no chance. I've never bought a scratchcard either. I've never been to Las Vegas. I have been one of the maddest punters you'll ever see and I've never been to Vegas because it's never interested me. I'm not a casino man. I once bought a mini casino set for an Arsenal tour and ran it, raking in the lads' money, but I don't want to sit inside at a roulette table, put all my money on red and spunk it in seconds. Do all my money on a spin in two seconds flat? Forget it. For me it isn't about an instant thrill or downer.

As the eighties turned into the nineties the betting markets exploded and I went with them, adding football, rugby, cricket and tennis to the horses and dogs because I wanted something that lasted longer than a couple of minutes. I wanted that buzz to be drawn out. Then I discovered American sport. American football, baseball and basketball are long, long games. That delicious uncertainty while the bet's still live in a tight game can last four to five hours. The euphoria or torture, depending on your view, of everything hanging on that bet for so long kept me only in that world and away from real life for an entire night, night after night. I wasn't fussed about anything else, focused only on the jeopardy, that mix of excitement and heart-stopping anxiety.

The process of the bet itself is the main attraction not the end result. If I won, I thought I had a bigger pot to win more. If I lost, I wanted it back so chased it. Those times I did win, within two days the bookies would have it all back and more. It was all about fantasies and fears, either the dream of winning big or digging yourself out of the deepest hole. Reality was the nightmare, when I would find myself with nothing left, all spent financially and emotionally.

With a wife and our first child on the way, we bought a bigger house. But I was always in debt, always chasing my tail, losing far bigger sums than I ever admitted at the time. We won the league again in 1991 and I couldn't afford to put carpet in the new house. I was a big part of that team, I missed only one game all season, scored 13 goals and was on decent wages by then. We won 24 games, so that was 24 win bonuses which were higher than my weekly salary, and the morning after we beat Manchester United in May to become champions, I got home to a house with stone floors and bare floorboards because I'd blown all my money. I got picked for England that year, had a nice boot endorsement contract as well and gambled the lot away. I used to have to pop round my mum and dad's just to get something to eat.

Given a choice I would always choose to gamble or, put it a better way, I could not resist the compulsion to bet. I'd kid myself, thinking, 'Never mind carpets, when I win I'll buy a yacht.' That was my mentality. Truth is, I never bought anything when I did win. I've got a mate who likes a small bet every weekend and if he wins £100 he'll buy himself something nice. He likes golf so will buy himself a driver, say, or a pair of new golf shoes. He'll spend it and he will always have something to show for it. But my first thought, even now, is, 'What? You're not going to have another bet and press it up?' Winning a bet to me made another, bigger bet possible. Win £5,000 and I'd want to press it up to £10,000 and so on and so on. It wasn't a nice holiday or a new car, it was a bigger stake next time. The dream was a never-ending betting spree, not the jackpot. I once won £20,000 and was sitting round my mum and dad's house that night with the cash, looking and feeling miserable. 'You've won all that money, why are you looking like that?' my mum asked. 'Because there's nothing else to bet on now. It's finished for the day.'

That would have been in the late eighties when 24/7 gambling wasn't possible because the betting shops were closed, I didn't have a credit account and there weren't the global markets there are today. Get to the last dog race and that was it. It was finished. I couldn't get a bet on a tennis match in Australia, say, back then. Now, it would take 10 seconds on a phone app. My uncle once said to me, 'Why do you gamble? Win or lose, even if you win 100 grand today, you're still having steak and chips for your tea. You ain't going to change.' He was right, I have always done it for the sheer sake of it. Materialistic things have never bothered me. I like a nice bed, a good telly and that's about it. It pleased me once, after all the heartache I'd caused when I was losing, to give my wife a good wedge of money when I won. A month later, though, and I was asking for it back because I'd lost everything else. And when she said, 'No' I'd learn the lesson . . . and never hand it over again the next time I won because I would know I'd need it back pretty soon.

I kept all these thoughts bottled up for years. I know it would be easier for a modern Premier League player with the same problems – plagued by debt, addiction and suicidal thoughts – to talk about it and be looked after. Talking is the first step and those who have come forward to speak about their mental health issues over the past twenty years have created a much better environment for understanding and acceptance. Back then I was convinced if I had gone and told someone the trouble I was in, the thoughts I was having, they would confirm my own suspicions and tell me that, yes, I was a horrible person and throw me out of football. There was so much fear. Players today, if they can be encouraged to talk about it, will find there is help available to nip it in the bud. I think that's great, I really do. I think it's amazing, coming from a time when a lot of people were terrified of admitting their addiction problems and were constantly worried about being thrown out of the game. Addiction is still doubted and condemned, cruelly mocked sometimes by a few loud and unkind people with made-up names on Twitter and Instagram. Society in general, though, recognises it for what it is, an illness.

There were some weeks in the early nineties when I was running up enormous gambling debts and when it got to 3 p.m. kick-off on a Saturday, as it usually was back then, it was the only time I could find any peace. I'd try to watch the 2.45 race on the TV in a tiny, stark room off the Highbury tunnel we called 'the Halfway House', where the players would traditionally huddle to have a team meeting away from the manager's ears, so it wasn't like all day Saturday was a sanctuary. I would also probably have had a punt on the 3.40 and would try to sneak in to check the result at half-time before going into the dressing room. It was on my mind all the time but not when I crossed that white line, pardon the pun. I was free for 45 minutes, then again after half-time, for another 45 minutes to do the thing I'd loved since the age of three. My obsessions with drinking and gambling were recent affairs by comparison. Football was my lifelong passion. It was pure release. Playing football was the only thing I could use to forget all those things I usually lost myself in to escape real life. Of all the mood altering or mind altering substances and pursuits I relied on to help me cope with life, football was always the best, the biggest high of the lot. I've tried so many things to change the way I feel but nothing comes close to winning trophies. The rush is phenomenal.

•

The 1990–91 Arsenal team was the best I played in. We were a much better team than the 1989 side. We scored loads of goals, three or more in a match 11 times, and hardly let any in. It wasn't 'one-nil to the Arsenal' or 'lucky Arsenal' or 'boring Arsenal' that year. Over 38 games we conceded 18 goals. It was unheard of – and the team with the next best defensive record in the league let 40 in. We lost one match all season in a massively more competitive league than the one we have now. David Seaman came in and he was just this huge presence in goal, he filled the nets, and Anders Limpar, on the left wing, was the only other signing.

Anders was a really good footballer. His feet were size five but they were just about the quickest I've ever seen. He was a joy to play with and it just clicked. Alan Smith won the Golden Boot for the second time in three years, Anders scored 11 and I had my best ever season as a goalscorer with 13. We don't get enough credit for what we achieved. The '89 team is always mentioned first because of the drama of Anfield. But that '91 team, we smashed opponents, we did the double over Liverpool who kept the title race going until the 37th game when we slaughtered Man Utd to win it, Smudge scoring a hat-trick. I scored in both matches against Liverpool, the one at Anfield in March in a 1–0 victory came from a 60-yard run, a one-two with Smudge, and – from further out but in other ways a bit like Mickey Thomas – having the belief and nerve to wait long enough for Bruce Grobbelaar to make his move before dinking it round him.

The game we lost was to Chelsea. I'm a Chelsea fan but they were crap that year. They wouldn't have even been in the top ten of teams we would have worried about. We had injuries that day, Tony Adams was still in prison for drink-driving and Mickey Thomas wound up having to fill in at centre-half. Even so, it was a shocker to get beaten. We could have been 'the Invincibles' and it still annoys me that if we had to lose it wasn't to one of the top teams. If it had been Liverpool who had beaten us, I'd half swallow it. Instead we got beaten by a team who were nowhere near us. I think the '91 side are the most underrated champions of the past forty years. We were a million miles better than two years earlier because we were tougher and cleverer after the experience of winning it the first time. We were also bang in our prime. To win it once is a fantastic achievement, but it's massive to win it again. No one can say you're not a great side if you win it twice.

I have to say, however unprofessional it looks by today's standards, the Tuesday Club played a part in that, which is why George never cracked down on it. It was a double-edged sword. It was not ideal that some of us would get paralytic together a couple of times a month in terms of weight and fitness but it was brilliant for team spirit. You need to be a proper team to win stuff. Some players didn't come out, some would come occasionally and not drink very much. That was never a problem. It wasn't a clique. There was no resentment between those who came along and those who didn't.

People will say you won because you could play and you had a good team, but if you don't have good team spirit you'll never win anything. If you're not running through that brick wall because you know everybody else will, you're not going to win, in my opinion. You have to respect one another even if you don't get on and be prepared to do everything you can because you know your mates are giving everything. You can put the best eleven players on the pitch but if they're all playing for themselves they will win nothing. We've seen enough talented football teams who don't win anything and you sit and scratch your head until you work out there are too many egos, too many I's. There weren't any I's in our team and the Tuesday Club, where we drank, took the piss out of each other and cried with laughter, helped build that bond. The fact that two of its leading members, Tony and me, turned out to be alcoholics was not because we'd drink together with the lads. Both of us already had alcoholism in our nature, we were heavy drinkers before the Tuesday Club and would find any excuse, when the mood took us, to drink with anyone and everyone.

The only disappointment that season was losing to Spurs in the FA Cup semi-final, which was played at Wembley. It was the match with Paul Gascoigne's 'worldie' of a free-kick, the one Dave Seaman kept apologising for, but while we all thought we were good enough to win the Double, Tottenham were brilliant in the first half and Gaz unstoppable. We battered them in the second half but let in a soft goal and couldn't come back.

My first boy, Charlie, was born during that season. I was twenty-two. Arsenal always wanted us to settle down, we were all married and had kids young. But getting married and having kids doesn't settle down addiction. It might stop it for a bit but, without treatment, you're soon back out there again doing what you've always done.

With Charlie's birth there wasn't even a pause. I arranged a loan from the bank to gamble with on the day he was born while Lorraine was in labour, spent most of the day in the bookies until they closed before turning up at the hospital and also stuck a load of bets on over the next few days, rather than do what most doting dads would do. I was in a panic about it all, the responsibility at such a young age, and sought an exit from the way I was feeling. Betting could preoccupy me in a way nothing else would. I never saw it as the cause of all my troubles. It was an escape from them.

Although I used to moan when the bookies shut for the night, when you're a compulsive gambler, everything is up for grabs. On the old team coaches there would be four chairs around a table, two forward facing, two looking backwards. We'd often play cards on away trips but when we'd had enough of that I'd make something up. I would be facing the way the driver's going and cars are whizzing past to my right. When you're betting on what colour the next car's going to be, you've got a problem. We did that all the time. Twenty quid on what colour car was next. How random is that? Another one, when we travelled up on a Friday, we'd buy *Country Life* and spread it out on the table, looking at the big houses that were in there for sale until we found one that said 'Price on Application'. We would all have a guess, chuck some money in the pot, use one of those early mobile phones as big as bricks to ring up the estate agent to ask the price and whoever was nearest won.

Something jolly that starts with twenty quid on the colour of the next car can escalate twenty years later into something quite crazy. When I was living alone in Sutton Coldfield when my second marriage ended, I would sit in and watch Noel Edmonds on *Deal or No Deal* in the afternoons. Me and my mate would ring each other up and go, 'Pick a box.' And we'd have £1,000 on whoever's box had the most money in, every single day. Sitting indoors, having a drink: 'Pick a box, a grand each.' And you'd either win or lose a grand every day. It was always a case of finding something to take me away from the way that I was feeling. You don't want to sit with yourself and your thoughts. When you've got something to bet on you're not worrying about anything else, not about the kids, the debt, the job, the marriage, the past or the future.

That's the way it always was, chasing a distraction, longing for excitement. In the March international break in 2021, I wasn't working on *Soccer Saturday* and I went to Homebase. I rang up my mate Noel from GA, who I talk to a lot. And I said, 'I've just been in Homebase on a Saturday afternoon. I'm fifty-three and I've never done that in my life ever.' I would either be playing football, working on Sky or punting like a maniac on a Saturday. I've finally come to a place where I'm not worried all the time I'm not working. At the age of fifty-three I did what normal, family people do for the first time. These days I go to Sainsbury's and do the weekly shop. Me, not my wife. Before my attitude was, 'Let's just get dinner for today' because I didn't want to waste any time by spending it in the real world, time I could be on the spaceship, drinking and gambling. Now I do stuff I've never done in my life and I love it because real life doesn't scare me anymore.

If you'd have asked me at twenty-three whether I was scared, I'd never have admitted it. Looking back, though, I was petrified but not of the thing that would have scared most people, the scale of my debts. With a four-year contract, even on wages which were a twentieth of what they would be today, there was always a way out, always a tomorrow. I was worrying that I was a terrible human being, not being able to control the desperation to bet and drink. My brain was never quiet. I did not understand what it was that was driving me and not understanding it tormented me. I didn't get hangovers as such, but the lack of a physical reaction to the buckets of beer and brandy I drank when I was out didn't spare me from the mental reaction, crushing shame and remorse. Why did I lose all our money? What sort of person would leave a toddler in the car on his own to rush into the bookies? Why was I so moody? Why did I shout at my wife? Why could I put my clown face on at work but be horrible at home? Why couldn't I stop when those who saw only bits and pieces of what I was doing thought I was pushing it too far? What if they knew everything? I didn't see addiction or illness in those frightening moments when I was on my own with only my thoughts, just an evil person looking back at me in the mirror. I had to be no good, I couldn't imagine any other explanation. That's what I thought for years. Insecurity and anxiety ate away at me and I blotted them out the best I could, medicating myself with the worst medicine.

•

Life terrified me but football was always all right. When you win the title the second time, you can easily get suckered into thinking it's going to last forever, but it was the last time I won it and I'd play on for another fifteen years and 650 games. We became a cup side, winning the FA and League Cups in 1993 and the Cup Winners' Cup a year later. George would tell you that he couldn't compete with the likes of Blackburn and Manchester United in terms of transfer fees and wages, so while everyone around us improved, we evolved into a more defensive team with a more direct approach in attack because the one big signing we did make, Ian Wright, was lethal and allowed us to rely on him to score and then we'd shut up shop. George was a brilliant tactician, so we could beat anyone in a one-off game, but over the course of a season in a title race, we just didn't have the consistency and depth anymore.

Ian had only been with us for a couple of weeks in 1991 when he was racially abused by Oldham fans at Boundary Park after he scored. I went over to him as they were saying those disgusting things. I was brought up in Harlesden, all my life I've lived in multi-racial communities. I can't have racism, I just can't, so while he was shouting at them and giving it back, I let them know how I felt, too. I'm so pleased that the issue is to the fore right now and that Sky is playing a big part in promoting the fight against it, but football has taken miles too long. When we were hauled up before the FA on disrepute charges for how we reacted at Oldham, it wasn't a case of, 'It's disgraceful what they said, we understand where you're coming from.' Not a bit of it. Their response was, 'You can't be doing that, you're getting fined.' And we were. It just shows you how far we've had to come.

What a player Wrighty was. Everyone talks about Jamie Vardy and what Jamie's done coming from non-League to win the Premier League with Leicester and play for England. Wrighty's story is like that. Everything about his life is absolutely phenomenal. He was a great goalscorer who loved the game. No footballer loved scoring more. People have short memories. As far as the modern game is concerned, what he achieved was all a long time ago. But it wasn't, not when you look at the history of football. There should be a film about him.

I've never known anyone so happy to come into training. Some days I'd sit there quietly getting changed and think, 'Oh fucking shut up, Wrighty. Turn it in.' With everything that was going on in my life, the contrast with him was extreme. He was so bubbly and loud all the time and I'd look at him thinking, 'Oh my God, not today. I've just dropped every bit of my wages.' Ian had all those qualities that you recognise at the time but maybe only majorly appreciate later. He's infectious, he energises people. His pleasure and joy come from a spirit that lifts you up. All kids should look at his career and his character as an inspiration, not just where he came from and what he achieved as a footballer but what he's doing now in the fight against racism. He's a great man.

We won nothing the first year he was with us, knocked out of the European Cup by Benfica and the FA Cup by Wrexham. The following year we won both domestic cups, beating Tottenham in the semi-final of the FA Cup at Wembley a fortnight before I scored and was man of the match in our 2–1 victory over Sheffield Wednesday in the Coca-Cola Cup final. I loved beating Tottenham two years after they'd ruined our chances of the Double. It was after that match that 'Doing the Merse' was born, when I ran over to some mates in the crowd and mimed chugging back pints. It was just a message to them, 'Let's go and have a drink, we've just beat Tottenham.' In fact I did it twice at Wembley, going for the encore after winning the Coca-Cola Cup. It was all over the papers on both occasions. When I came out of rehab the first time in January 1995, I hated that image of me. It made me cringe. Even worse, I let the magazine *Loaded* take one of Charlie mimicking me, which I thought was a great laugh at the time but hated myself for encouraging it after the first bout of therapy.

Yet I've signed more pictures of me doing The Merse than any other. In Arsenal terms, it is iconic. There I am, tongue out, busted tooth and a perm that had gone terribly wrong. I look like Cher. For a long time after rehab, I would reflect on those days with horror and shame, annoyed that the image the world had of me was that of a lairy piss-head. When I became clean and sober for the first time, I was embarrassed by the 'Wild Thing'. But I have a better perspective on it now. In 1995, I would regularly say the Serenity Prayer I learnt in treatment: 'God, grant me the serenity to accept the things I cannot change, courage to change the things I can, and wisdom to know the difference.' It was only later that I really got it. Now it's like a mantra for me. I say it dozens and dozens of times a day, hundreds of times on the days I struggle. I know I can't change the past and am not as harsh on the younger me as I was when I was fresh and raw from rehab. When I see 'The Merse' now, I'm glad I'm not like that anymore but I don't hate the person I used to be.

I do regret something about it, though. I look back now and see the pictures and I think, 'Wow, I got man of the match and scored in the League Cup final, does it get any better than that?' A few weeks later we won the FA Cup, beating Sheffield Wednesday again, this time in a replay. I also won the league in 1989 and 1991 and the Cup Winners' Cup final in 1994. Everything I won was while I was at the height of my addictions. The one memory I have and can recall, as clear as the day it happened, was winning promotion at Portsmouth. Every other time I won something, all I was worried about was what I was doing next. I could not live in the moment. It was always, 'Where are we going tonight, then? Big piss-up tonight! Winning that brings a big bonus. That means punting.'

Every thought I had after the game was about what it meant for drinking and gambling. The significance of what we achieved went straight over my head. You hear a lot of rock stars say they play a big concert and they come off and they've got a massive high and they don't know what to do with themselves. That was me. I would have loved to have gone home and taken it all in and savoured it. All the pictures, medals, man of the match awards back then, my attitude was 'Fuck that, let's get in and have a drink.' I don't mean that disrespectfully but it's the truth of how I was. What a shame! I had such highs on the football pitch that when I came off it I wanted it to carry on. The only way I could make it continue was by drinking and gambling, and by 1993 even they weren't doing the business for me like they used to do. I just felt empty most of the time. I was looking for something else. Finding it almost cost me my sanity, my family, my job and ultimately my life.

6

THE MOUSETRAP

Terry Venables saw right through me straightaway.

He wasn't the first to work out the trouble I was in, the trouble I could cause him, but he was the first to do something about it. Graham Taylor, his predecessor, nailed me with a comment when England were on a tour of the United States after Arsenal had won both cups in 1993, one of those pointed remarks said as if he didn't want me to hear it but actually did. 'Merson, he's a good player,' he said. 'Only trouble is, you don't know what will happen next, whether he'll be carried out of a taxi legless. I want him in and around the box but unless I put a pint of lager in the middle of the goal, then no chance.' But despite that, Graham kept picking me. Terry took one hard look at me when he became England coach in 1994 and bombed me out of the squad.

I was called up for Terry's second and third games, friendlies against Greece and Norway in May 1994, and we met up as usual on the Sunday evening after the FA Cup final at Burnham Beeches Hotel. Back then we would park up, check in and head for the bar to catch up with the lads, have a few drinks and then go to bed. But when every other player and eventually the barman left for upstairs, I wasn't done and I carried on drinking until 3 a.m., climbing over the bar to pull my own pints. Someone on Terry's staff had stayed up to keep an eye on me and must have told him. He did pick me on the Tuesday against Greece and I played the whole game, which we won 5–0. I had a shocker, though, and was Greece's best player. The next day he asked me for a chat and said, 'You won't be involved with the squad again while I'm England manager.' He was true to his word. I didn't even make the bench for the Norway match and that was it, completely out of the picture. I wish I could say I was distraught when he told me, but I was so far gone I was defiant: more weeks off, more time for drinking, gambling and my latest addiction.

The way he did it, I couldn't hold a grudge against him because of his honesty. I'd much rather that than him being the kind of manager who would say, 'See you next time' and you would never see them again. I knew where I stood. I didn't have to sit there and put Ceefax on, which is how we found out if we'd been picked, thinking, 'Hold on a minute. I didn't get in again.' He had been given first-hand reports of me drinking away like a maniac and thought, 'No, I'm not taking a chance.' He had been around the scene for thirty-five years, had the public on his side after Graham resigned and had the experience and confidence to deal with me. I have no problem with that. Yes, he wasn't so ruthless with other players in the squad who had addiction issues, but mine were far more obvious than theirs. He might have seen Tony Adams drunk, but no one knew he was an alcoholic. Besides, he was his captain, a great defender and a great leader. Similarly, you can't put me in the same bracket as Paul Gascoigne. Gazza was a one-off, one of the best players in the world. However good I was, I wasn't that. You need world-class players in international football and you can't sacrifice two of them on principle. No manager would. England weren't relying on me, they had options in all the positions I covered – Teddy Sheringham, Steve McManaman, Darren Anderton, Rob Lee and Steve Stone. It was a strong statement for him to make at the start of his reign: someone is doing well at his club but you say, 'No, no more.' It sends a tough message to the other players. Now they're thinking, 'Fuck! Merse is out and he isn't coming back.' I understood why he did it at the time and when I used to bump into him when I was back on track, we had a laugh about it.

If that had been the end of my England days after 14 caps, it would have been a disappointment because I didn't give myself a chance, didn't do justice to my talent. When I'm asked to sum up my England career I'd say, only half-jokingly, with what I was doing off the pitch it was a miracle I played once. I should be knighted . . .

I was in a bad place during those years and some of the long trips we went on, I was in bits, betting like a lunatic, drinking whenever there was an opportunity. Yet I think back to my debut against Germany in September 1991 and I remember the feeling of pride. There is no bigger accolade as a footballer than to play for your country in a nation where it's the national game. As we stood singing 'God Save the Queen' I thought it was the ultimate honour and, looking at my family's faces in the crowd, knew that they felt it too.

I came on for the last 20 minutes of that 1–0 defeat by the world champions, Taylor's first loss after a year in the job. I replaced John Salako down the right and put in a couple of nice crosses. I didn't play again until the following March, making my full debut against Czechoslovakia when we looked like Coventry, playing in all sky blue. It's a hell of a feeling when you're selected to start a game. You are the best player in your position, on that day at least, of everyone in the country and you're playing against the crème de la crème of another country. I scored the first equaliser with a right-foot shot from the edge of the box in a 2–2 draw and, though I started only one more game, I was picked for the Euro '92 squad.

That tournament is remembered more for the violence at England games in Sweden than for what we did on the pitch because we were crap. It came a bit out of the blue to be told I was starting the first game against Denmark on the right. I did okay but picked up an ankle injury and we clung on for a 0–0. I had an x-ray and had to miss the next game against France, another goalless draw, but was fit enough to be on the bench for the third match against the hosts, a match in which we needed a win to be sure of qualification for the semi-finals or a high-scoring draw if the France–Denmark game went our way. I came on as a substitute at 1–1 with 15 minutes to go, but that was instantly forgotten because 15 minutes earlier Graham had sent on Alan Smith for the captain, Gary Lineker. You should have seen the other substitutes' eyebrows. They all shot up and we winced as we exchanged glances. It wasn't a controversial call, it was a downright mistake. Some managers under pressure make poor decisions and that was one of the worst. Of course, bring Alan on. Smudge was one of the best forwards I ever played with, but even Alan will tell you, bringing off one of England's greatest goalscorers when you need a goal to win and go through is madness. I'd have sent Alan on without hesitation. He was a goalscorer, Golden Boot winner in two out of three seasons, one of the most underrated players in top-flight history. But you leave Gary Lineker on the pitch. Even if you have to take the goalie off, you leave Gary on the pitch. We needed to score. Instead Thomas Brolin scored for them, we were knocked out, the *Sun* turned Taylor into a turnip and his confidence and authority were ruined. He was never the same again.

Graham was unlucky with injuries. He lost Alan Shearer, Stuart Pearce and Gazza for long periods, but tactically he was all over the place. He never gave Ian Wright much of a chance and there was never any continuity from one match to the next. He liked organisation and patterns and once made us watch an hour of the opposition taking throw-ins before a match to show us how we could exploit the moment we had eleven on the field and they had only ten. But they only had ten men for a second. During the qualifiers, Des Walker lost his 'You'll never beat Des Walker' brilliance at the back and we really started to struggle. Graham was a decent man and tried his best to make sure the lads wouldn't be bored witless holed up in Burnham Beeches for days on end by organising trips to the theatre, games rooms and the like. But players can smell when a manager's in trouble and, although it isn't done nastily, they start taking liberties.

·

In the summer of 1993, we went to the United States for a four-team tournament which was supposed to be a taster for the following year's World Cup. We arrived in Boston a week after a trip when we drew with Poland and lost to Norway, making qualification tricky and unlikely. In all my drinking days, it was the best trip I'd ever been on. A proper beano. I didn't want it to end. I'm only grateful that the camera crew who were filming the Cutting Edge documentary that turned into *Graham Taylor: The Impossible Job* weren't with us. I know it became a great film for the fans but, whether deliberately or not, they stitched up Graham and his staff with the editing, making Phil Neal and Lawrie McMenemy look like nodding dogs. I can't think of a single occasion in my career when a No 2 or coach would openly disagree with his boss in front of the players, never mind the cameras. It didn't distort reality in that sense, but they didn't find room in the film for all the positive parts of Phil's work on the training ground or Lawrie's skilful man-management. I had enough problems of my own and didn't pay the cameras much attention. I was living inside my own head at that time, I didn't take much notice. I could have walked into a room of 100 people I knew but felt entirely alone.

I drank to forget about the gambling debts and I drank, as I always had, to fit in, to give me the confidence to talk to people. Drinking takes the anxiety away at the start but after a while it feeds it. So, when you sober up the next day, you not only remember everything you drank to forget about, you're on edge. When I was on my own in the room when I was with the England squad, the old insecurity would come flooding back. I would think, 'What am I doing with these players? They're miles better than me. I don't deserve this. I shouldn't be here.' Even though the manager was pick-ing me, I'd always have in the back of my mind, 'I'm not that good.' I know now that a lot of people suffer from imposter syndrome, they expect to be found out. The problem in football is, being found out comes in a brutal and public way. The papers can give you a five out of ten and write, 'He shouldn't be in the squad.' Or the crowd can get on your back. Tony Adams got labelled a donkey for scoring an own goal at Old Trafford in 1989 and a tabloid stuck big ears on his picture on the back page. One of England's greatest centre-backs was still getting 'Eeyores' at away grounds six years later.

If people now say to me, 'You were a brilliant player' I say, 'Thank you.' Before I'd say, 'No, no I wasn't that good.' Someone might say, 'You're a legend' and when I was ill it made me cringe. I used to think, 'Oh my God. If you only knew what I was doing, you'd know I'm not a good man.'

Now I know that I was ill and not a bad person, I can take a compliment. I can think, 'Yeah, I could play. I could do things other players couldn't do and I see players today who couldn't do what I could do.' So I give myself the credit I couldn't allow myself in the past. People in football who have worked with me, I think, would tell you, 'He's not right in the head, there's something wrong with him.' But I would also expect them to say, 'He could play. He had vision.' Even now, I can see things on the pitch when I'm watching games that I don't think people see. There's only really Kevin de Bruyne in the Premier League who surprises me and does things I can't see. I watch him and think, 'Where's he seen that? How on earth did he spot that run, how did he pick that pass?' I wish I had accepted the praise in the past and believed in myself more. It would have made a world of difference to my career and, more importantly, my life.

I hadn't played in Poland or Norway and still wasn't in the side for the opening match of the US Cup against the hosts, which we lost 2–0. The papers called England 'Norse Manure' after the shambles in Oslo, now we were 'Planks' beaten by 'Yanks'. Alexi Lalas scored their second goal and came over to our bench to do a massive knee slide to celebrate right in front of me. George Graham had brought him in on trial at Arsenal and had asked me to look after him and show him around. Not that I took him out anywhere. I used to sit in the bar of the Noke in St Albans where he was staying and get pissed while he got out his guitar and sang. He was a good lad, but George sent him packing because he used to kick anything that moved in training. After scoring against us, he was keen to have the last laugh. I sat there mouthing 'Fuck off' at him under my breath as he rubbed it in. Being beaten by the USA was a new low without someone who was a better guitar player than he was a footballer taking the piss.

From Boston we flew to Washington to play Brazil. We weren't allowed out of the hotel the first night so got hammered in the bar, but when everyone sloped off to bed, I wanted more and walked out of the hotel in my England tracksuit to find somewhere, anywhere, to carry on. I sneaked out, turned left, walked a couple of blocks and found a total dive with a smashed up jukebox and someone passed out at the bar. I quite happily necked a few more beers while talking bollocks to the barman and eventually stumbled out to make my way back to the hotel. Before I could get there I staggered into two huge blokes who were yelling and about to try to rip each other's heads off. Sober, I'd have run a mile, but pissed I decided I'd be the peacemaker, slurring some soppy stuff about how they should make up and that violence was never the answer. They must have thought I was a nutcase and both turned on me, shouting and pushing me, so I legged it, making my way back to the hotel as quickly as I could. I was laughing with the lads about it the following morning at breakfast when we were joined by two FBI agents, who were going to brief us about what we should and shouldn't do in DC before we left the hotel supposedly for the first time. They told us about Washington being not just the actual capital but also the murder capital of the USA. 'Always turn right when you leave,' one of them said. 'Do not turn left. Down there,' he said, 'is the murder hotspot of the most dangerous city in America. You will find yourself in serious trouble if you turn left.' Everyone's jaws hit the floor as they stared at me. I don't know how I stopped myself being sick. I could easily have been shot. Booze gives you a feeling of indestructibility but the following morning your stomach lurches when you realise how close to the edge of disaster you were.

I stayed in the hotel after that until we went out following our 1–1 draw with Brazil. I got on for the last five minutes of that game and we celebrated a good performance and result in Georgetown, a posh part of the city, definitely not to the left of the hotel. I knocked back loads of beers and decided it would be funny to climb on top of a stretch limo that was parked outside the bar and dance on top of it. I was arseholed and thought it was a great laugh when the alarm went off and the lads were cheering. Loads of people were staring at me and Graham Taylor was mortified, coming over and saying, 'Please Paul, get down. You must. Please get down.' I refused and stayed up there until I slipped off, falling heavily and hitting my head on the kerb. It was like I didn't care anymore, like I was wild. I thought I was having the time of my life. The next morning he called me into his room and said, 'Enough is enough, Paul. I'm going to send you home.'

I knew he couldn't afford any more grief, though. 'You don't want to be doing that, do you?' I said. 'That's the last thing you need to be doing. If I'm sent home, everyone will want to know why you can't control us and there will be uproar in the papers.' The pressure he was under meant it was hard for him to crack the whip. I look back now and think how I exploited that and I know it wasn't fair or clever, but I was in a bad way, completely out of control. He kept me on the tour and we headed to Michigan, which is where he made that comment about the only way to motivate me was by sticking a pint in the area.

The strangest thing of all, though, was that after taking me to Katowice, Oslo, Boston and Washington and giving me all of seven minutes on the field, despite what I'd done and said, despite saying he would have to put a beer in the box to get me to perform, he picked me for the final match of the US Cup in Detroit against Germany. And, against all logic, it was the best I ever played in an England shirt. It's amazing how fine the margins are between being a nearly-man, which I was in international football, and a success. I made a really good chance for David Platt in that match with a perfect diagonal over the defence but he headed it wide. Then, after flicking it over their left-back, I hit a dipping half-volley from 30 yards that brought a worldie of a fingertip save from Bodo Illgner.

A couple of months later I started our penultimate World Cup qualifying match against Holland in Rotterdam which we needed a draw from, at worst, to give us a slim chance of making it to the finals. I had a shot in the first-half from outside the area that faded round the post at the last second and after Ronnie Koeman, who should have been sent off earlier, put them 1–0 up, I hit the inside of the post from a 25-yard free-kick and the ball squirted across the goal-line and stayed out. If either that effort against Germany had crept under the bar or the free-kick against Holland had rebounded the other side of the line and we'd gone on to qualify for USA '94, people would still be saying, 'What about Paul Merson's goal, eh?' It's weird how close it can be. I did okay for England considering how I was feeling and the way I was living. But between being okay and being remembered as a good England player, for me, came down to a few inches.

We went to Bologna to play San Marino in the last qualifier. We won 7–1 after Stuart Pearce's mistake gave them a shock lead. I didn't get off the bench and, with us missing out on the World Cup, Graham resigned shortly afterwards. Apart from the Greece game the following May under Terry, that was me done with England for almost three years. I could tell myself that not playing for England would give me more time for Arsenal, or laugh it off with the lads, saying international breaks would give me loads of time off for boozing and betting. I wasn't thinking straight enough to realise what an opportunity I'd wasted. We were hosting Euro '96, we didn't have to qualify and the way Terry transformed how England played, focusing on passing, good touch and width, would have suited me down to the ground. But I'd blown any chance of being involved. I couldn't think that far ahead in May 1994. I was in serious trouble.

•

The gambling had become ridiculous. Ray Parlour will tell you a story from the days when we roomed together. I'd be sitting on the bed before an away game and put Teletext on. They used to have eight dog races back then. I'd say 'Who do you fancy?' And he'd look at me and say, 'You what?' I'd tell him to pick a number and when he did I'd phone up the bookies and put £1,000 on, say, trap three in the 8.06 at Walthamstow. And we'd wait for the result to flash up. Absolute madness. Win, or more usually lose, I'd go, 'Pick another number.' And I'd dump another grand. I was just sitting there doing that not to be bored, so I wouldn't have to think about myself. Niall Quinn remembers me ringing him up late on a Sunday when I didn't want my wife to know I was betting on four American Football games. I whispered to ask him to look up the scores on Ceefax, I needed two results to go right to climb out of a deep, deep hole, three to get ahead. All four went down.

Credit accounts helped me lose the plot. Everything becomes unreal. It's like a game. The money is Monopoly money. You walk into a betting shop with £10,000 in cash and hand it over the counter for a bet. Even in fifties that's 200 notes, which make a pretty thick wedge. However ill you are, that's hard to do. Why do you think all these betting firms embraced telephone and online accounts so much? It's because in the punters' heads, there's a sense that it's a game, it's not real. It's like in those quiz shows where they offer you a chance to keep what you've already won or go for the big money and they show you a briefcase full of notes. Even if you know the answer, you're still going to be intimidated by looking at the cash, so most people stick with what they've got. If you were at home, you'd be shouting the answer at the telly. Because the money's there, it's psychologically harder. Even on *Who Wants to be a Millionaire?* when they show you the million pound cheque, that's more intimidating than just saying the number out loud. It's the other way with punting – you can think that the stake doesn't really exist because you can't see it, you haven't held it, you haven't physically taken it out of the bank and handed it over to someone else. It's not real until they start coming after you for what you owe. And what you owe just mushrooms because when you're a compulsive gambler you're always going to chase your losses. You're not going to stop. You're not stopping when you're winning, you're not stopping when you're losing.

The gambling fuelled the drinking, the drinking fuelled the gambling. And now there was no respite, whereas before, at 10 o'clock at night, everything stopped. Without credit you couldn't phone up for a bet. Unless you were at the dogs or a summer evening horserace meeting, you weren't getting a bet on late. When I started playing the pubs used to shut at 3 p.m. And then reopen at 6 p.m. There would always be a break. With the gambling, as soon as a certain time came, that would be it. Not anymore. I would ring up the bookie pissed and make some crazy bets. Ten grand on the Eurovision Song Contest, five grand on the world bowls, five grand on a Lithuanian basketball match on a Monday morning. When you ring up to bet on a Lithuanian basketball match, the bookies aren't worried you've gone mad, they're not concerned for your wellbeing. They treat you as a rational human being when you're doing irrational things, as long as it suits them. I knew something about football, American football and the horses but even then I couldn't win. What did I know about Eurovision, rugby league, bowls, basketball? Nothing. I just wanted to have a bet. All the bookies are worried about when you're having a bet on something as weird as that, is whether you've got the edge. How are you going to have the edge on a basketball game when you don't even know what colours the teams are in? There was a Gamble Aware advert from a couple of years ago and the line was: 'You don't even know what colour kit they wear.' That's so, so true. If you gave me my money back on every bet I've had when I didn't know what colours the teams were in, I'd be minted.

What do you do when the things you do to take you away from the world stop doing it for you? My instinct was not to confront why I couldn't cope with life but to find another escape. You would have had to be a fool or blind not to notice a blizzard of cocaine blowing through the kinds of pubs and clubs I knocked about in around London and

St Albans back then. It wasn't blatant, but if you knew the signs, it was obvious. My attitude when I was out with my mates or among Arsenal fans was to steer clear. I thought what it would do to me was something like dope or what I'd heard about Ecstasy and acid. The last thing I wanted was a trip. I was scared of everyday life but the thought of hallucinating and being stuck seeing dancing elephants for the rest of my life was horrible. My reaction, then, when offered it for the first time at the Mousetrap, a lively pub in Borehamwood, was to politely decline. This was February 1994 and I shouldn't have even been there in the first place. There was a mix-up over where I was supposed to be meeting my mate and he didn't show up. I was flying solo, surrounded by Arsenal fans who kept buying me drinks. My mate didn't have a mobile phone, so there was no way of sorting out where he was. And, as I've said, when I was in a place with my drinking head on, I was in for the night.

I've always got on well with fans. I never really got any stick, apart from at Walsall. I've never been out and fans have started on me. Quite the opposite. I think many of them related to me: they saw me as one of their own, someone who loved football, liked a drink and a bet. I was nothing different to a lot of them behind the goal. I dressed like them, I spoke like them and, on the surface, it seemed as if I thought like them. So, when one of them asked me if I wanted a line, that was probably their thinking – he's just like us. Although I turned the offer down and carried on drinking, I couldn't stop thinking about it over the next few days. I didn't say to myself, 'Do you know what, I think I'll try a bit of that. I fancy having a line.' I'd tell myself instead, the next Saturday night I can, 'I'm going back to the Mousetrap, I really like that pub'. There was nothing special about the place at all. No legitimate reason to go back there rather than the dozens of other boozers I liked. Thinking about the pub in terms of the atmosphere and the 'top-drawer banter' was a way of not admitting to myself the real attraction, which was unspoken in my head. It's hard to express – I knew but I didn't acknowledge it, like it was at the back of my mind, safely kept away from the front.

I hadn't been playing well, I hadn't scored for five months and George had dropped me to the bench for six games. Not long after that first night in the Mousetrap I was back in the side and scored a really good goal against Everton at Goodison Park, chipping Neville Southall, who was huge and still one of the best keepers around, from 25 yards. I knew I was going to party hard that night. Five months without a goal, months of bad form – of course I was going out. As soon as we got back to London Colney from Merseyside, I jumped in my car and drove a couple of miles south to Borehamwood, ordered a lager top and scanned the room looking for the bloke who had offered me cocaine. He wasn't there at first, so I just settled in for a night of heavy drinking. But later, I saw him and I felt a real rush of excitement. We got talking about the match and when he offered me a line this time I could barely have followed him into the toilets any quicker.

That decision led me towards ten months of hell. When I came forward at the end of the year, confessed, begged for help and went into treatment, it suited everybody to play down the amount of cocaine I stuck up my nose from February to November 1994. I think I said I'd spent about £2,000 on it on my own and shared some more. That works out at about 40 wraps of a gram each. It was way, way more than that. At its worst I was doing a couple of grams down the pub, and I was out all the time, then many more at home, on my own, sitting in the dark gambling, drinking and snorting.

I knew how serious it was but I was ashamed, so I said it was £2,000. You have to remember how addiction was covered in the newspapers back then. We were weak people or sleazy people or 'junkies' or criminals, sometimes all four. I don't think Arsenal and the FA could stomach being associated with any of that talk of dealers, drug dens and pub toilets. They encouraged me not to publicly acknowledge the real extent of it. Plus many in the game, pardon the phrase, had looked down their noses when the news about Maradona's addiction to cocaine and his failed drugs test for a stimulant at the 1994 World Cup came to light. They liked to tell themselves that it couldn't happen here.

When I came out of treatment, journalists wrote that they understood it was the least of my problems, hinting that I might have exaggerated how hooked on it I was because addiction gave me an 'excuse' to go into treatment; whereas casual, recreational use would have brought me no understanding from the authorities and a long ban. 'The newspaper which paid Merson for his initial confessions,' one wrote, 'vastly overstated his drug use.' It was quite the opposite. We underplayed it. Let me be quite clear: I have an addictive personality. It's not the drink or the gambling or the drugs in themselves. It's in my head. It could have been food or sex or anything. I always went all-in. I took cocaine in such quantities that I was physically and psychologically addicted to it. I wasn't hoovering up loads of grams all the time, not at first. But what started with the chopping out of lines in a toilet cubicle in a Hertfordshire pub ended with me driven to the brink of madness, alone at home, all wiped out in every sense, broke, twitchy, paranoid, suicidal, naked, crumpled in the corner, crying my eyes out, utterly helpless.

7

'I'M REALLY STRUGGLING. I NEED HELP.'

The first snort of cocaine took effect virtually straightaway.

My heart was racing and pumping the blood at a million miles an hour as I walked back towards the bar. The thing that struck me was how I *felt*. It had taken the edge off all the pints I had drunk. I felt sharp and, weirdly to me, super confident, not just happy to talk to anyone but keen to talk to *everyone*. There were none of the usual nerves. I was talking to complete strangers, chatting to women, when I would usually struggle to overcome my shyness. I necked more and more pints of lager top, which barely touched the sides. But they weren't the reason I kept popping back to the toilet. I wanted another line, then another and another. It was like gambling – I placed my first bet at sixteen and within a quarter of an hour of walking into the bookies I'd lost a month's wages. With drinking, too, I'd had one Pernod and black and didn't stop until the room was spinning and I spewed my guts up. Again, it took only a few moments for me to be hooked on the way coke made me feel. And when I woke up the following morning after three hours' sleep, I was surprised to feel as right as rain. Given I'd drunk almost twice as much as I normally would have done, which was already a lot, I thought, 'Hmm. This is all right. It isn't as dangerous as everyone makes out.' How wrong can you be?

I thought that way because I hadn't realised that I was different, that I was ill. 'Normal' people can have a bet and not empty their bank accounts. 'Normal' people can have a couple of drinks and go home when they'd said they would, not 10 hours later pissed out of their minds. And, although it's illegal, we know that 'normal' people can even dabble with drugs without craving it all the time. That wasn't me. I wanted another night out on cocaine as soon as I could. I started out by keeping it to some Saturday nights after the match, looking forward to it all week, but when the season ended, it got much, much worse.

There was no mandatory, random drug testing in the Premier League back then. That all came in for the 1995–96 season after Diego Maradona was kicked out of the 1994 World Cup which coincided with my year on drugs. Had I been tested at any point from February onwards, although I wasn't dabbling every week at first, I would have failed and probably been thrown out of football. It didn't take long for George Graham to receive a letter from a concerned fan who wrote that he had 'spotted Paul Merson buying drugs in my local pub. His behaviour is quite unacceptable for a professional sportsman.' George called me in and asked me what the hell was going on. But being devious is second nature when you're all-in with an addiction. I was lucky, too, because a snout had once reported me for being pissed and completely out of order in a West End club on a night when George knew I was in Marbella with the rest of the squad. I exploited that case of mistaken identity for all it was worth on more than one occasion. 'C'mon, Gaffer,' I said. 'It's Spurs fans winding you up, trying to drop me in it. Remember that time we were in Spain . . .'

He believed me and even apologised for bringing it up. I was playing well, too, so there was less to be suspicious about. After scoring with that chip against Everton, I got the only goal of the match the following week at Highbury to beat Blackburn, who were second and 13 points ahead of us in fourth, then hit the late equaliser a couple of weeks after that with a half-volley into the roof of the net against the leaders Manchester United. I finished March with the winner in a 1–0 victory over Liverpool. Cocaine isn't performance enhancing, of course it isn't. It's a killer. But for a few weeks, I was flying high, riding the buzz before the crash.

Once Charlie and Ben, my first two boys, were sleeping through the night I began to go out more than usual and would sneak back in near enough to dawn and sleep in the spare bedroom to avoid awkward questions or a row with Lorraine. Among my circle of cocaine users, I stood out, not because I was Billy Big Bollocks and flash, that was something I never was, and not even because I played for Arsenal and England, because I never behaved as if I was different to them. What alarmed them was how much I'd take in one snort and how often I would want a top up, because I was constantly chasing the high. 'Oh my God,' someone once said. 'You can't do it like that. You have got to calm down.' But I couldn't. I would want the biggest rush I could get, then sit there all fidgety back in the bar and drink loads to settle my heart-rate down before heading back to the toilets for another fat line. My heart was on a rollercoaster all night, lurching up and swooping down the big dipper. It's a wonder it didn't just stop and pack in, leaving me dead of a heart attack at the age of twenty-six. I had looked at it as something to soften the blow of the gambling debts when the booze stopped working, but now I had three things working at once, each of them an attempt to distract me from the mess the others made of me.

While the season was still in full swing, you would think there would be some restraint. There wasn't. The number of games and trips abroad in our run to the Cup Winners' Cup final meant there should have been fewer opportunities for big nights, but I took any chance that I could. I am bewildered that I managed to keep it together as long as I did. Even before I'd started on cocaine, I'd lost seven grand betting on us to beat Odense in the home leg of our first-round tie. We were 1–7 for a home victory so I would have won a grand, but they scored a late equaliser and although we went through I sat in the dressing room feeling thoroughly sick. 'Why do I keep doing this?' I asked myself. 'Why?' I couldn't find an answer.

George was in his element in that competition, loving the tactical battles. Every team talk mentioned 'patience, possession, positivity', but that was the only thing that stayed the same. He came up with all types of different strategies – we suffocated Torino with a defensive masterclass in the quarter-final and surprised Paris Saint-Germain in the semi-final first leg by attacking them. I sat deep on the left in a 4–5–1 in Turin and played tucked alongside Ian Wright behind Alan Smith in a Christmas tree formation at Parc des Princes.

I missed the second, home leg against PSG because UEFA competitions did have mandatory drugs tests and I was scared to death. The match was on a Thursday and I'd been out the Monday night for a drink, one thing led to another and I ended up off my face. I was rough for a few days and swerved the match with 'tonsillitis', which was the only time I missed a game because of drugs. Did I feel guilty about that? Of course I did, but I wasn't thinking straight. I was up to my neck in debt, had been depressed for months, booze was making me unwell, I was barely eating and, with the adrenaline from the gear as well, I had lost pounds in weight. The drugs were sending me round the bend. I was moody, my behaviour was making my family unhappy, I was making myself unhappy. There were loads of lows, a few artificially created highs, but very little joy. I was lost.

One-nil to the Arsenal did the trick at Highbury against PSG and we went to Copenhagen for the final against Parma as huge underdogs. Wrighty was suspended, John Jensen and Martin Keown injured, Michael Thomas and David Rocastle had long since been sold and our opponents had

Thomas Brolin, Faustino Asprilla and Gianfranco Zola in attack. I must have been more sensible in the run-up to the final. I don't think I risked it. Although I was experiencing the first signs of paranoia, it didn't become full-blown until much later in the year. But I'd lost my form again, was too weak to push myself hard in training and I'm sure I only made the team because we had a small squad and too many injuries.

George's approach was as brilliant as it had ever been, the equal of Anfield in 1989, if not better given we had Steve Morrow and Ian Selley in central midfield because of all the absentees. The noise in Copenhagen was amazing. Arsenal outnumbered Parma fans three to one, it seemed, and made a racket, lifting us when we knew the odds were stacked heavily against us. We knew we couldn't outplay them so we were never going to try. But we out-thought them, worked our bollocks off and, though they battered us, we scored a goal after 20 minutes and clung on for dear life. Alan Smith scored it, a wonderful left-foot half-volley after Lorenzo Minotti made a balls-up of a clearance. Lee Dixon had followed a training-ground routine word for word. From a throw-in he gave it to Smudger, who knocked it back and Dicko fired a ball towards the box that was coming to me. Minotti flew in with a bicycle kick before I could get there but hooked it straight to Alan. He took it on his chest, let it bounce and rifled it just inside the right post from 20 yards. It was a fantastic goal and great for Alan, who'd had to adapt since we signed Wrighty. The positions Alan used to take in the box, he found, were now occupied by Ian so he had to change his runs and come away from the places where the best opportunities to nick a goal have always come. It was nice for him to be an out and out goalscoring No 9 again on the big stage rather than doing all the donkey work that often goes unrewarded.

From that point on, we were under siege. The back four and David Seaman were magnificent, the wide players, me and Kevin Campbell, tucked in to make a five in midfield and Paul Davis, who George had sent into exile for more than a year after an argument, showed his class with his passing and the way he organised the kids, Selley and Morrow, alongside him. That was the night 'One-nil to the Arsenal' really took off as a song and we bellowed it out with the fans when we received the cup. It was my fifth medal in five years as a first-team player, and the last of my career. There was no big piss-up to celebrate in Copenhagen because we had the last match of the season against Newcastle a couple of days later. With Wrighty available for that, I knew I wouldn't be playing so used our day off when we flew home to feed the three addictions. I knew I couldn't be seen out before a match so I shut the curtains, scanned the *Racing Post* and got seriously stuck into betting and bingeing on drink and drugs. Just as the first two had long since stopped being only a social thing, now the same happened with drugs. I was withdrawing into myself entirely, certain that I couldn't trust anyone. I was living two lives.

In one life, at the end of the season I went away with Lorraine and my two boys on holiday after being told my England career was over by Terry Venables and didn't touch drugs. In the other, on the night I returned I made some excuse to Lorraine about needing to deliver some presents we'd bought to a friend, went round his house and got straight back on it until the early morning. She put my long absences that summer down to my selfishness rather than a drug problem. I would disappear on benders for a couple of days, hang out in some dodgy places, kip round a mate's or crash out in the spare room, hunkering down in front of the telly on my own in the middle of the night doing gram after gram when she was asleep or when I'd deliberately engineered a row so she would go off with the kids to her parents and I could get the house to myself. I was absent even when I was there. I'd wander away from the dinner table to check the results on Teletext when we had friends round or walk out of a restaurant before anyone had finished to find a payphone to ring the bookie and find out how my bets were getting on.

·

One summer evening when the family were away, I'd taken so much coke that I'd actually run out, having been punting and boozing all day. I was wired, though, couldn't come down and was desperate for more. When I wasn't off my face I knew that I had a major problem. I couldn't get enough of it. I exposed myself to all sorts of danger to get it, hanging out with drug buddies I barely knew and dealers, running up debts with them, and laying myself open to being ripped off, beaten up or blackmailed. That night, when I couldn't get any from the regular contacts, I headed down to the Middlesex and Herts Country Club. It wasn't as grand as it sounds but even so it was a swanky nightclub in Harrow. Still, no one normal would have got in wearing a pair of flip-flops, Bermuda shorts and a T-shirt, not in 1994. I bullshitted a bouncer who recognised me, telling him I had to give my mate his house keys and promised to be back in a second. He let me in and off I went, looking like a fish up a tree among the blokes in Versace shirts and girls in their Saturday night best.

I shuffled straight to the dancefloor and started approaching people, asking 'Got any gear?' I was too far gone, red eyes, runny nose, brain haywire, to go up to only those people who looked like they might have some. I asked anyone and everyone, couples, groups of girls dancing round their handbags. I could actually hear people saying, 'That's Paul Merson after gear. Fucking hell.' It's only when you come out the other side that you realise how crazy it was. It couldn't happen now. If there had been camera phones back then it would have been nailed on impossible. I would have been caught in 10 minutes. I was on it for ten months. Eventually I scored a couple of grams, went home and stuck them up my nose, oblivious to what dozens of people must have thought of me.

The same was true when the season started. I began taking absurd risks. I wonder now whether it was because I knew I couldn't make myself stop, so I was subconsciously courting being found out to force me to find help. When we were on a pre-season tour of Sweden, Lee Dixon told us one afternoon about a mate of his who worked at the *News of the World* and a story they were about to break on a Premier League footballer. Apparently, he'd been 'up to loads of bad stuff and they've been trailing him for months'. He said he didn't know who it was and I even joined in speculating about his identity and what he'd been up to. If it had been me, and now I think it could have been, any one of 100 people could have tipped them off.

I had started kicking on after closing time at the Mousetrap by going to a pub in Smithfield Market, where the meat porters drank, which was open through the night. I'd be on my own drinking at the bar and snorting in the toilets, hail a black cab at 8 a.m. to take me up to training and even have a couple of big hits from a wrap of coke in the back, in full view of the cabbie staring at me in disbelief in the mirror. In my head, I fronted all the repercussions out – even if they report me, they'll have no proof, my word against his. I was that far gone I thought I was untouchable and yet when I came down, I felt totally vulnerable. The swing from one to the other would be extreme and I'd start to feel crushing paranoia about being followed, about being a target.

The walls were closing in. I played seven of the first eight league games but we were struggling and I was awful. We

Aged 9, and Brent Schools' Under-11 leading goalscorer.

Professional Sport/Popperfoto via Getty Images

Above. In the Anfield dressing room with Perry Groves and Alan Smith. We'd just beaten Liverpool with a last-gasp goal to claim the 1988-89 First Division title. It was a JFK moment for football fans.

Below. The notorious goal celebration.

Getty Images/Shaun Botterill

Right. I co-operated with the *Mirror* because I'd been advised to do a story to avoid a feeding frenzy among all the newspapers. I also did it to pay off my gambling debts and fund my rehab.

Below, left. The press conference before I went into rehab. To tell you the truth, I didn't want to go. I didn't want to be away from the kids and Lorraine or miss Christmas at home. I didn't want to be on my own among strangers.

Below, right. Fresh out of rehab, the trigger for the tears at the press conference was talking about what a typical day inside the centre had been like.

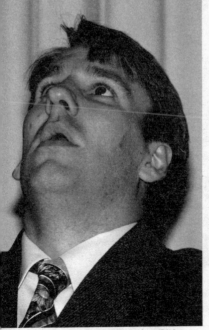

Above. Gazza is the nicest bloke you could wish to meet. Life was lived at a hundred miles an hour but that used to be the way I wanted it when we were at Middlesbrough together.

Left. I was named Villa's 'Player of the Season' twice in four seasons, and we reached the FA Cup final in 2000, losing to Chelsea.

Right. With my Pompey boss Harry Redknapp after securing promotion to the top flight in April 2003. It was the most enjoyable season of my career.

Below. On the touchline with Walsall in November 2005. Management is hard enough when you're well. It occupies your thoughts all of the time. But when you're ill? Really, I had no chance.

Mirrorpix/Reach Licensing

Action Images/Keith Williams Livepic

Mark Leech/Offside via Getty Images

Owen Humphreys/PA Archive/PA Images

Above. Letting fly for England against Germany in a friendly at Wembley in 1991.

Left. With my great mate and fellow Gooner Tony Adams, this time in England training clobber in Sweden in 1998.

Above. When *Harry's Heroes: The Full English* came out in March 2019, it allowed me to see the wreckage my gambling and drinking had left, how powerless I was in front of them.

Below. I was in a very different place by the time we filmed *Harry's Heroes: Euro Having a Laugh.* I confronted my old mate 'Razor' Ruddock about his drinking: if I didn't care, I wouldn't have bothered.

Above. My second home, *Soccer Saturday*. With Jeff, Matt, Phil and Charlie.

Right. A note of desperation I wrote to myself in August 2020, when I relapsed. I accept that this is not going away.

30ᵗʰ AUG 2020
I NEED TO STOP GAMBLING
I Love my wife and
Kids and I'm So happy
with them, when I was
in orlando with my wife
and 2 little Childnen it
was the happiest I have
been in years, Cos I wasnt
gambling I hate myself
when I gamble I hate it
please help me Cos
I need to pay everyone
back and get my wife
and kids a home please
GOD HELP ME

Left. Wedding day with Kate. She's the only person who fully understands me.

won two, lost four and drew one of them. I broke my nose in a match against Leeds but it didn't stop me having a heavy night on the gear before it was reset and all strapped up. I'm sure the doctor who looked up my nose before taking the temporary dressing off a couple of days later could see what I'd been doing. I was getting used to the kind of look he gave me as people's minds ticked over, adding the evidence of cocaine use right before their eyes to the fact that I was Paul Merson of Arsenal and England, two things that shouldn't go together. It wasn't disbelief but shock. Disgust.

I had bookies chasing me, dealers chasing me. I settled one cocaine debt by handing over my Arsenal blazer as payment and reporting it as stolen to the club. My mind was racing at a million miles an hour and I started to think that if I played well and had my face plastered all over the papers, some random bloke, who didn't know who I was but had seen me on drugs, would go to the papers.

Paranoia and suicidal thoughts took over. I was convinced someone was hunting me down and it started taking me an hour to get to work on what should have been a 10-minute journey. I would try to shake them, doing U-turns, double-backs and pulling over to see if a car 'on my tail' would go past. If I saw a car I didn't recognise on our road, I'd cook up all sorts of nightmare scenarios – that it was a dealer coming after me with a baseball bat or a journalist who'd got the story and was about to confront me with it. I had dark thoughts about being killed by one and stuck on the front page of a tabloid by the other. If anyone was at home with me, I'd make them go out and discover who was in the car. If I was on my own, I'd hide in the back of the house until they'd gone. I couldn't get any rest. Feelings of doom and being exposed invaded my dreams. Who was going to grass me up? I feared it could be anyone. I was a nervous wreck. But I couldn't stop. In September, when I was injured, I ran up enormous debts, lost for days in a vicious circle: place a bet, snort a line, sink a can of beer. Rinse and repeat. The days blurred into one.

I couldn't go on but, given I didn't know how to get myself out of it, I went on. If I looked for help and the club found out, I was convinced they would either have me sectioned or sacked. I was frightened of Lorraine finding out, so I did my best to avoid her, coming home late if at all. I was frightened of everyone who cared for me finding out. That's the swing: from 'Fuck it! I couldn't care less what anyone thinks' when you're high to guilt, shame and 'I'm the worst person in the world' when you're not. They're the two sides of the coin when you're as far gone as I was. The only obvious solution, my brain was telling me, was to kill myself. I would be out driving and see a lorry coming towards me on the other side of the road and I would think, 'Pull in front of it, just do it.' For weeks, that thought was in there all the time: 'This is the only way it's going to end.' But something within me fought to keep the steering wheel straight.

By the beginning of November, I was in crisis. I took so much cocaine one Saturday night that I couldn't get my heart rate down. I stumbled out of the Mousetrap and into the car park, gulping down fresh air, but it didn't do any good because I was hyperventilating, just like the panic attacks when I was a kid. I sank to my knees, certain I was going to die. I managed to get myself home and, with that addict's bravado, was back on it at the next opportunity.

I was scared witless again during our Cup Winners' Cup tie against Odense at Highbury when it felt like my heart was going to explode. It was like a vice squeezing the breath out of me. I couldn't run because I couldn't breathe. I have no idea how I got through the game. I couldn't concentrate on what was happening in the match at all. I'd always been fearless on the pitch and fearful in every other part of my life. Now I was afraid while playing. I didn't stop then, but the end was near.

It took a week after the Odense game. One last week of excess on the brink of madness at the end of which Lorraine, spooked by a tip-off about the scale of my gambling debts, had spoken to George Graham about her concerns. She was six months pregnant with our third boy, Sam, at the time. She must have been out of her mind with worry at what I'd become. We'd met at school and she had no experience whatsoever of the gambling and drinking scene. For years I convinced her my behaviour was the norm for young men of my background, especially footballers. But as she grew older and I became wilder, she was at her wit's end with worry about what I'd become. She didn't know the half of it, of course, yet that was enough to know I was in serious danger. When she told me what she had done, I was angry, frightened, cornered but still went out on a five-hour drink and drugs bender. That night when I got home to an empty house, I cowered in a corner with nothing on, bawling my eyes out, begging for help. I didn't want to live like this and I realised I didn't want to die like this either. My head was about as fucked up as it could possibly be, strung out on booze and coke and fear and paranoia. I was on my knees. I couldn't beat it. I had to surrender. Through the tears I could finally accept that I was on the floor and desperately needed a hand-up. I had to come clean.

Not to Lorraine at first. I didn't want to scare her off. I drove to Highbury to speak to George and the managing director, Ken Friar. Both were well aware I was in trouble but, having spoken to my wife, thought it was restricted to massive gambling debts which had pushed me towards far too many booze binges for comfort. Their jaws hit the floor when I told them how much I owed to bookies, legitimate ones and the other kind, and mates I'd borrowed money off as a last resort when my credit ran out. 'I'm really struggling,' I said. 'I need help.' Then I told them about the drugs. Obviously, they were shocked. Blown away. They were worried, disappointed but brilliant. There was no anger. Ken was very calm. 'Right,' he said. 'We're going to get you help.' The sense of relief was enormous. I knew it was my last chance, but it was a chance all the same.

It took about a fortnight for them to work out what to do, the first week of which I spent in the gym trying to get some fitness back. They spoke to the FA straightaway and their press officer, Mike Parry, who went on to be a talk-SPORT presenter, advised that my best course was to tell my story to a newspaper and go into rehab. By that time I already had a sponsor, Steve Jacobs, a friend of many Arsenal players who had been in recovery from compulsive gambling for a number of years. He worked as a counsellor and it was him I turned to after telling the club. He took me to my first Gamblers Anonymous meeting, which was a struggle. My shyness meant I couldn't say too much more at that point other than my gambling had got out of hand and the debts were overwhelming me.

In those two weeks, I white-knuckled abstinence from gambling, drinking and drugs, which was unbelievably tough. If you asked on *Family Fortunes* what cocaine does to people, I bet the top answer would be 'Keeps you awake' and the next that it lets you drink all night. But the worst thing, the paranoia, is not so well known. It affected me for years. It didn't just go when I stopped taking it, not even when I went through treatment. My head was screwed up for ages and, when mixed with my natural, high anxiety, made me nervous and suspicious for a long, long time.

I had taken the first small step towards putting my recovery on firmer ground for success by that trip to GA, but for those couple of weeks I was only physically holding the addictions at bay. I hadn't confronted what made me do it and I hadn't begun to think about how to live my life on its own terms without needing these dangerous, powerful ways of escaping. I threw myself back into being a good father, went training and stayed at home in the evenings. No one apart from senior people at Arsenal and the FA knew until a deal was brokered and I agreed to speak to the *Daily Mirror*. They'd been told the gist of what I was going to say, made an offer and I spoke to them on a Thursday afternoon after training, telling them about an addiction to gambling and alcohol that had spiralled into cocaine use. The FA insisted that I keep the extent of the drug addiction vague, because if I revealed the truth, they would be under intense pressure to ban me for life. Even the level of drug abuse I did admit to was sensational enough and, as the paper prepared to go to print with thousands of words about me to appear the following morning, me and Lorraine were flying to France to get out of the country before it hit the newsstands.

I co-operated with the *Mirror* because I'd been advised to do a story to avoid a feeding frenzy among all the newspapers. I also did it to pay off my gambling debts and fund my rehab, but I didn't know what they wanted me to say until I sat down with them, nor that they would stick me on the front page with the headline: 'I'm hooked on cocaine.' They whisked us away to Paris and then Cannes with two *Mirror* reporters because they needed follow-up stories and didn't want the other newspapers to spoil their exclusive. Incredibly, I also needed to get away so I could tell Lorraine. That's where I told her about the drugs: on the flight to Paris. 'Try and keep your wife, that's the most important thing' were George Graham's parting words to me the night we flew out. And she did stay despite everything I told her about the debts and the cocaine. I was choked telling her, but the worst moment came a couple of days later when one of the reporters took me aside and insisted I told my pregnant wife that a couple of weeks earlier, on my very last night out on gear, I'd had a one-night stand. I didn't think anyone would make me do that just for some extra sauce for their readers. As if the drugs weren't enough, it felt like they wanted to twist the knife. I think, to be fair, they were afraid another paper would get the story but it was brutal. They took us to the south of France to a hideaway, pulled me into a room and said, 'Right, you've got to tell her you've cheated.'

That was the most sick I'd felt. Why inflict pain needlessly on her after already hurting her so badly? When I had the one-night stand, I was out of my head, completely and utterly off my nut. When you're drinking and taking drugs on that scale, you don't care what you're doing. And because you don't care about yourself, you're not going to care about the ones you love. The woman I went with, they told me she would sell her story but she was not the kind. When I bumped into her again, many years later, she said to me, 'I'd never have sold a story about you. Never.'

The papers back then were ruthless. Once, when they were about to run a story about me chatting up a woman when I was unwell and drunk, they came round the house demanding a comment. I'm not proud of it but when I was younger and playing for Arsenal and unwell it was different. There were opportunities to stray and I wasn't always as good as I should have been. I begged them not to run it, not to hurt my wife and kids. I said, 'C'mon, mate. My wife's having a baby, it'll really hurt her.' But the reporter's attitude wasn't, 'We know where you're coming from Paul, but this is our job and we have to run it.' He couldn't give a shit. He actually said that. He took great pleasure in it all. 'You're fucked,' he said.

The sportswriters were all right. I'd always talk to the press if I was rubbish in the game or fantastic. I wasn't one of those players who would only talk if they had a good game. I'd be honest and always find time. I was fortunate with them; most sports journalists were fair. The split between how sports and news journalists treated me hit me in the face when I was writing a football column for the *News of the World* and was being paid to do so, while at the same time the front pages were printing stories about my private life. I would say to the journalist I worked with on the column, 'I work for this paper, surely they wouldn't do that?' But they did. They couldn't, as the man said, care less. What we know now about what they got up to with phone hacking and putting private detectives on you, I reckon, 100 per cent, they were after me for a long time.

Telling your story to one paper makes you an enemy of the others and when we flew back from France, there was a scrum of photographers and reporters at the airport, jostling, swearing and screaming questions. We went from there to Highbury to meet George and Ken to hear what had been decided for me by the club and the FA and the upshot was that I was to do a press conference the following day and once that was over, go home, pack a bag and head to a residential rehab facility, the Marchwood Priory Hospital near Southampton.

I sat alongside Graham Kelly of the FA, Gordon Taylor of the PFA and George to speak to the press, confessing my sins under intense questions. Some of the most pointed ones criticised me for cashing in with the newspaper exclusive and implied that a recreational user might use 'addiction' as a way of getting off the hook for drug-taking. I felt fragile and vulnerable but George, who knew what I'd been through and how hard I was finding it to read the prepared statement fluently under the glare of the TV lights and camera flashes, how difficult it was to answer the sneering tone of some of the questions, was magnificent. When I felt like breaking down, he squeezed my leg and it gave me such a lift.

To tell you the truth, I didn't want to go into rehab. I didn't want to be away from the kids and Lorraine or miss Christmas at home. I didn't want to be on my own among strangers. I wasn't stupid. I knew I had a mega gambling issue but I didn't know I was an alcoholic and addicted to cocaine. I thought because gambling was the trigger or, with my compulsive gambler's head on, that losing was the trigger, if I could control that with GA then I wouldn't need to drink or take drugs to distract me from the core problem. I had no choice, though. The FA made that perfectly clear. Either go in, have successful treatment while serving an indefinite ban and then submit to frequent drug and alcohol tests for a probation period of eighteen months or I'd never play football again.

When you put it like that . . . Reluctantly, I went in and stayed for six weeks. I entered Marchwood thinking I was addicted to one thing and left knowing I was addicted to three. But I was clean and sober and keeping a lid on the urge to gamble for the first time in more than ten years.

8

THE INVISIBLE ENEMY

Day one in rehab. All alone. No wife and kids. No mum and dad. No friends or team-mates. No boss, no crowd, no football.

But also no pub, no dealer, no bookie.

I was in Marchwood for six weeks in total, much of which has blurred in my memory. There were so many tears, as I was coaxed out of my shell and learnt to trust the therapy and the people I was with, that it's hard to remember specific details more than the emotions of coming to terms with so much trauma. I listened and I learnt to talk, eventually coming to enjoy the discovery of why I did what I did. That phrase 'spilling your guts', was what it was like. You emptied yourself in therapy, telling everyone what you'd done, reflecting on it and analysing what motivated the behaviour that had brought you to your knees. As well as the tears and remorse, there were uplifting moments of support from fellow addicts, the doctors and staff as we built a bond. But the paranoia was still raging at times and when someone was allowed to leave and a new person joined, I was worried until I'd sussed them out properly that they might have been a reporter looking to record everything I said and stitch me up in the papers. I must admit I confronted a newcomer with my suspicions only to be put in my place when she revealed she had no idea who I was or how I could possibly be famous.

I didn't need to dry out at the clinic. I hadn't taken any gear for three weeks and I hadn't had a drink since a couple of glasses of wine with dinner in France with the *Daily Mirror*. I tried to work on my fitness, running most days, and was grateful for mixed doubles tennis matches with my doctor's wife and her friends. I remember you could never forget it was an institution – the furniture in our rooms was screwed to the floor, we weren't allowed any sharp objects and the TV room, where everyone went in the evenings, was full of chain-smokers, puffing away and staring straight ahead with their chairs pointed at the telly. There were loads of meetings, starting with the police – who only cautioned me for drug use, much to my relief as I feared harsher treatment – and with Gamblers Anonymous, Alcoholics Anonymous and Narcotics Anonymous, as well as individual and group therapy. I was diagnosed as an alcoholic and cocaine addict early on after they went through the assessment form I'd filled in and I began the first step of recovery.

I had a hard time digesting that I was addicted to drink and drugs. The picture in my mind of what alcoholism and drug addiction looked like didn't fit with what I'd been doing. I could go days without drinking and I could steer clear of drugs if I wasn't on a mad gambling binge and pissed out of my head. It was there that I learnt the definition of alcoholism isn't someone who drinks virtually 24/7, apart from when they're passed out; it is someone who can't stop once they have started. When I drank back then and later when I relapsed, I never really went out with bad intentions to stay out all night, get into trouble and turn my phone off when my wife rang. Every night I thought I was in control, but one drink inevitably led to another. My destination was always oblivion. Being told that in hospital and figuring out that my behaviour fitted that pattern was a real eye-opener. Loads of things fell into place.

The main word I learnt about coping with addiction was 'surrender'. I had to surrender and accept that I suffered from a sickness, to substitute 'bad' and 'weak' for 'ill'. I'm not a mad and bad person, I'm an ill person. That's the thing that people who are still in the grip of addiction need to understand. They don't know they're ill, they think they're horrible failures with no willpower. And they're not. Far from it. But until you know you're an addict, thinking you're evil does terrible damage to your mental health. I'd say ninety-nine per cent of unaware compulsive gamblers and alcoholics don't know that their self-hatred is being driven by their addiction. They simply think they're weak. 'I've just worked all week and I've done all our wages,' they could think. 'We've got no money. We can't pay the rent. Oh my God, what am I going to do with my wife and kids now we haven't got the money to pay the rent?' Those thoughts are telling you that you're a hateful human being. But you're not; it's the illness that's a bastard, not you.

It's hard to understand that you have compulsions, and it's especially difficult for other people to accept it. I couldn't count how many times over the years I've heard the argument that the gambling, drinking and drug taking were 'your choice'. As I've grown older I've been able to say that it wasn't my choice. I didn't have free will. I was driven and I didn't know what I was dealing with. But when you're younger and you don't know you're an addict, when you're drinking like a mad man, gambling like a lunatic and snorting bags of coke like someone with a death wish, you just think you're greedy and selfish and you can't stop. You've got 'a Millwall head on': no one likes me and I don't care. In fact, I don't like anybody either. That's how you think when you're in a spiral to the bottom.

When I came out of rehab I had learnt to use tools to hold alcoholism and gambling down for a long time, but it was a struggle. There was no magic cure, that much was clear. I was twenty-six, a kid. Understanding you have addictions is one thing but over time new thoughts battle back against that. The voice of the addictions tells you now that you're well, if you do it sensibly this time, where's the harm? Some friends will be able to drink and gamble normally, have a couple of quid on the first goalscorer or have three pints and go home. If they can, why can't you? At twenty-six you might have another sixty years. That's a long slog without the things that you've relied on for all your adult life.

It's 'my choice' now, knowing what I know. I know what I am and I know the nature of my addictions. At fifty-three,

I choose not to drink and have a bet but when I left March-wood to go home after successful treatment in January 1995, my recovery wasn't totally secure. Now I know it never really is. What I didn't properly appreciate when I came out was that relapse is a normal part of recovery for most multiple addicts. Not many give up everything at the first attempt for all time. Not knowing that means that if you do get drawn back into those old habits, the shame and the guilt are even worse than before. 'You should know better,' you tell your-self as you beat yourself up. It took a lot longer than those six weeks for me to accept the addiction's not in the drink or the bet or the drug. The addiction is in my head. It's an inside job.

Even in rehab, the main focus was on the drink and the drugs, not the gambling so much. It wasn't like in America where the issue of compulsive gambling was more widely accepted in those days as thankfully it now is here. I don't think the FA and the PFA were all that interested in that problem. Drugs was the big scandal that pushed them to insist on rehab and when I came out, after being assessed by FA doctors as being well enough to go home and resume my career, I was forced to do a press conference where gambling was hardly mentioned. It was all, 'Merse, you can't have another drink, another line.' No journalist made a point of saying, 'Merse, you can't have another bet' even though, playing it down, the FA and PFA issued a statement saying for me drugs were 'only a minimal problem'. I don't think all the betting was taken seriously, because if you're not a compulsive gambler it's hard to imagine the chemical reaction in my brain that gave me a rush when I put a bet on. You can imagine changing your mood with something you put into your body from the outside, drink and drugs, and how you can get hooked on them. But gambling is invisible. That's one of the reasons why it's the worst; and because you can't explain it properly to people with no experience of it themselves.

•

I haven't touched drugs since 1994. I know what cocaine did to me and I'll never do it again. Part of my brain recognises how dangerous and bad that was: the paranoia, the heart beating at a gazillion miles an hour, chasing the high in all sorts of grim and dangerous places. I don't know how my brain is wired but for twenty-seven years it has recognised that taking cocaine is not good for me, to steer well clear. It fascinates me that it's the one addiction I've been able to control successfully for the longest time.

I do have an image of how my addictions work on my memory. With gambling, I see two wires that are joined together carelessly in my head and every now and then they flicker and spark and come away from each other. And when they do that, I forget how bad gambling is for me. As soon as the join breaks, the pain of how quickly and completely it always defeats me is gone and my brain tells me, 'C'mon, Paul. It ain't that bad.' With cocaine, I see it as being plugged in, the fuse is working and I would never do it again because

I remember how horrible it was. I've been around it enough times since then. If you know the signs, you'd spot how widespread it has been in pubs and clubs for thirty years but I'd never entertain doing it again. I've been drunk and around people who have been on it and it has never interested me.

It's the one penny that has dropped. When I was drinking and having fun and someone put it in front of me, I could and did say 'No'. I've never been fearful of relapsing. It's like I know it's in the past. But gambling and drink have also brought me to my knees and although I was dry and didn't bet for more than three years after coming out of Marchwood, the addictions did drag me back under. I lost millions of pounds, drinking and gambling have cost me heartache, everything, my houses, cars, my job at Walsall and my entire pension fund. And yet I've been back to them a million times.

'Cocaine = bad' – the pain, paranoia, suicidal thoughts and panic about having a heart attack – is embedded in my head. The gambling is on a fuse that works some of the time, it's lit . . . lit . . . lit and all's well . . . and then the wires become detached. Living as I do now, I try to take everything one day at a time and the longer I can go without being tempted back towards addictive behaviour, the wiring feels gradually more secure, like the cocaine one. Offered cocaine, my brain automatically flashes warning signs and I instinctively walk away. Offered ten grand credit, I want my brain to naturally say, 'That's not good' and turn it down. That is where I would like to get to with gambling, for it to be plugged in.

That actually happened to me in 2014. I was out. I'd had a drink. Someone I met offered to introduce me to someone who would give me ten grand credit. By the way, in my old world there are quite a few people out there who prey on compulsive gamblers, exploit us and use us as a source of easy money, pushing credit to the addict, knowing full well we'd end up in their debt. That day the fuses weren't joined. 'I'll have some of that,' I thought. 'I could nick a few quid here.' Straightaway I put £7,000 on Wales to beat Andorra at 1–7. I thought, 'I'm nicking a grand.' Unlike before with the Eurovision Song Contest or Lithuanian basketball, my thinking here was: act rationally like a professional gambler, someone whose head is straight. Don't look for a big win, take the scraps on the favourites and by the end of the month he's going to owe me a lot of money. I remember the game, Gareth Bale scored in the last 10 minutes and Wales won 2–1. You've nicked a grand. Job done. Trouble is you start like that, but it always finishes the same way. By the end of the month I had to give the bloke ten grand.

The thing that helped more than anything with staying off drugs after I came out of rehab was that I was tested three times a week. I got so used to it that I would show the inexperienced dope-testers how to do it properly and keep everything sterile. It helped that I knew they were coming three times a week. The FA said to me that I'd be banned forever if I tested positive, so there was no messing about. It was ingrained. It was quite easy and I don't really know if it would have been as easy without the regular testing. I stayed away from the kind of places where drugs were rife. That was my way of dealing with them. There's a saying in AA: if you keep hanging round the barber's all week, you're eventually going to have a haircut. It's the same for me with pubs and betting shops. I steer clear. If you knock around drinking gaffs and places where people take drugs when first out of rehab, where conversations focus on drink and drugs so you're talking about them and thinking about them, by the end of a week you're going to be back on it again.

The questioning at the press conference arranged by the FA on the day I came out of treatment was not the trigger for the tears. That came when I spoke about what a typical day inside the centre had been like. It all hit me at that moment and George put his arm around me and spoke on my behalf until I could hold it together. It was a bit like therapy – frankness is encouraged and I spoke truthfully and with no glossing over any criticism of myself. It was shown live on Sky and a photo of me dabbing the tears away was all over the front pages the following day. Some reporters were fine, others stuck the boot in, calling me 'a mug not a martyr' and 'the celebrity who got off lightly'. I never claimed to be a martyr or wanted to be seen as one, but I wasn't surprised by the hostility, which seemed more driven by me talking to the *Mirror* than a reaction to my illness and recovery. I felt bad when I was in treatment and read that a player at a League Two club had got done for smoking dope. And they threw him out. I was fuming because unlike the way Arsenal helped me, there was no 'Wait a minute, let's think about the player. Why has he done that? There has to be a reason why he would do that.' No, they sacked him because it was convenient. They probably already wanted him out.

I had to change everything about the way I'd led my life over the past year and had a whole new routine of training and meetings, NA in Wembley, GA and AA in St Albans as well as spending quality, engaged time with the boys and Lorraine. There was no hostility in the dressing room. The lads had been brilliant throughout. I had withdrawn from them in the months leading up to the final meltdown because I was petrified of them finding out about my drug problem. But so many rang and wrote to me, with such tolerant, encouraging words that they brought a lump to my throat. They also treated me like the old me, keeping me up to date with everything that was going on in the dressing room, bringing banter and normality to my unreal situation. I'll always be grateful to them for that and they welcomed me back with real warmth. I had a couple of weeks' training, during which I answered all their questions about what had happened and the changes I had made to my life. No more Tuesday Club for me, no more card schools and I think many of them from that point on kept an eye on me, making sure I was never put in dangerous situations surrounded by temptation.

•

I had to wait for the FA to allow me to start playing again and they agreed after eighteen days that I could resume my career. George named me as sub for the European Super Cup first leg against AC Milan at Highbury. It was an amazing night. My dad, who had been to the games when I was in treatment, said the supporters were right behind me. The fans sang my name when I warmed up and there was a huge roar when I went on. I am where I am today with the public because of how I behaved. People relate to me. I very rarely got stick playing away from home. Everywhere I went there would be a bunch of people in the crowd who would think, 'Yeah, he's made mistakes but he's exactly the same as us except he plays football. Deep down I bet he's no different.' It was that reception and the way fans continued to treat me, still calling me 'Magic Man', still chanting my name, that helped me overcome my nervousness and allowed me to enjoy playing again. I had to run across the pitch from the dugout to the right wing to take up my position and Paolo Maldini gave me a pat and said, 'Welcome back.' One of the greatest players of all time saying that to me was incredible. I had a lump in my throat. After all the shit I'd been through, it felt like a fresh start for the new me.

I was back in the starting XI for the next Premier League match against Sheffield Wednesday and I was ever-present from then until the end of the following season. I was sober and went on a blinding run of form. When it was only gambling, going out to play for me was heaven for an hour and a half, an escape. No one was going to run on the pitch and say, 'You owe this.' By the time I was being battered by all three addictions, it was affecting my form. If a player's having serious problems and you could take them away, it would improve their game by eighty per cent. Look at Harry Maguire after he was arrested in Greece last summer. When he came back he looked as if he had the weight of the world on his shoulders and he was making mistakes. He took his problems on to the pitch. Remember Leeds United's Lee Bowyer and Jonathan Woodgate when they were arrested for affray? Bowyer played out of his skin, you'd never guess anything was bothering him. Woodgate went completely the other way, couldn't play at all. Stopping the drink and the drugs let me get back to my best at work and in life. It was no coincidence that I played my best football from 1995 to 2003, particularly my four years at Aston Villa, when I was drug-free and, bar a couple of lapses, off the drink. Tony Adams will tell you he got sober because of me. He'd seen me and how my life had turned around, how I'd be coming in, bright eyed and bushy tailed. Tony got that message. When he hit rock bottom he knew there was another way to live . . . and if I could do it, so could he.

My return to form was too late to save George who was sacked three weeks into my comeback. They got rid of him for accepting payments from Rune Hauge, an agent who had sorted the deals that brought John Jensen and Pal Lydersen to Highbury and also because our league form had been patchy for four years. The papers had been chipping away at him with the revelations for a couple of weeks, but it was still a huge shock when he went. He had stood by me at my darkest time but there was nothing I could do to help him at his lowest point. It also sparked fears about what the new manager would think of me – apart from that handful of games at Brentford, I'd only ever played for George – and how I would feel if he didn't rate me or understand my problems. I'd had enough of a wild ride in my life. At that moment I craved stability and that was what the boss represented.

Stewart Houston, his No 2, replaced him as caretaker and while we continued to do well in Europe, our league form remained poor. Having had nothing but George and his strictness with organisation, discipline and tactics on the pitch for nine years, it wasn't surprising that the players took their foot off the gas. However kind he was to me, 'Son of George', when I most needed it, he would have ripped our heads off if we had ever slackened off. Under Stewart it was still 'shut the lines and show people inside', 'back four squeeze the pitch' but without the same intensity. That fear had gone and for many, who'd been terrorised by George during wage negotiations, been given earache when he spotted a mistake or sent into exile after they'd had a disagreement, there was a sense of freedom.

Defending the Cup Winners' Cup we'd won in Copenhagen, we beat Auxerre away to go through to a semi-final against Sampdoria and took a 3–2 lead to Genoa for the second leg. Off the pitch, it hadn't been plain sailing all the way since I came out of rehab. I was attending meetings, going back to Marchwood for therapy, enjoying my time with the family and evenings of takeaways and the telly rather than the pubs and clubs of the old days. But when I watched a rugby match on TV the urge to have a bet, 'One punt won't hurt', gripped me for hours and it took loads of effort not to do it. I would talk to my counsellor or my sponsor on the phone and I'd understand that the compulsion was still there and the tricks it would play. They were a great help, genuine people I could rely on, yet it was a battle, not constant but a regular one. I had a bad game against West Ham in March and, for the first time after I'd had a stinker in my career, I didn't get pissed to get away from the negative feelings. It felt very strange. There were many of those little trials but going to meetings, especially GA, was the key to overcoming the urges. If I missed one when work intervened like when we played the away legs in Europe, I could get very down and doubtful. You have to work at it: go to your meetings, talk, don't have any secrets.

After extra-time in the second leg of the semi-final against Sampdoria it was 5–5 on aggregate and we moved on to a penalty shootout. We went first and were 3–2 up when I walked up to take the fifth. If I scored, we won, simple as that. I had visions of the back pages the following morning, all the glowing headlines about redemption and thinking back, perhaps that would have been my iconic recovery image, like Tony Adams against Everton in 1998. But I missed it. I said afterwards that what I'd been through with the addictions and rehab had given me a different perspective on life and I could take missing a penalty in my stride. That was total bollocks. Trudging back to the halfway line my head really went, I couldn't hear the crowd or the consoling words of the lads, only the voice in my head. 'If we don't win this, I've let everybody down. What is the point? I could score penalties when I was drinking and taking drugs. If we lose I'm back on it. Right back on it.'

I was panicking like hell as Attilio Lombardo walked up to take their fifth. If he scored, we'd go to sudden death. Luckily enough, Dave Seaman saved it and saved me. I knew as soon as he pulled it off that I'd had the narrowest of escapes. I would have blamed myself and said the two most dangerous words an addict can ever say: 'Fuck it.' My thought process changed the moment Spunky clawed the ball away. I wasn't one of the first to jump on top of him, I was too overcome by a wave of relief and realisation how fragile recovery is sometimes. It was the worst moment I'd gone through when sober and somehow I'd survived it. That was the only time that something happening on the field pushed me close to triggering a relapse.

I was once asked whether Nayim's winning goal from 50 yards for Real Zaragoza in the last seconds of extra time in the final in Paris was the thing that pushed me closest to the edge. 'That must have been a punishing blow for you?' It wasn't at all, not in terms of fearing I'd turn back to the old ways to get over it. I know football well enough to recognise it was a great goal. He had tried something similar earlier in the game from a bit closer in. He had the vision to spot Dave Seaman just that crucial few yards further out that opened up the tightest of opportunities and the skill to score a worldie of a goal from the halfway line. When you are beaten by a great goal, you can swallow it. I hate losing, don't get me wrong, but when I see such quality I hold my hands up and say, 'That's the game. It was a special goal.' I was gutted, of course, but we had lost as a team. Our luck had finally run out. Against Sampdoria I had felt personally responsible but in Paris we suffered together. And as for blaming David Seaman? He blames himself, but it was such an unbelievable strike, the ball went so high before dipping at the last moment, I don't think he could have saved it. In any case, we wouldn't have got there without him and I doubt I'd be here today if I'd relapsed after only a couple of months. I honestly think Dave saved my life.

The club appointed Bruce Rioch as manager in the summer and also announced the signing of David Platt from Sampdoria and Dennis Bergkamp from Inter Milan. Dennis was Arsenal's best signing and the finest footballer I ever played with. He had everything apart from express pace – the best touch in the game, composure, a brilliant passer, hard as nails with a touch of nastiness and a vision like no other. Glenn Hoddle always said he liked players who 'could see pictures'; no one saw pictures quicker than Dennis, where the space was, where the runner was heading, what the defender would do. In pre-season in Norway, a few of us were walking back to the hotel after training and saying, 'They must be brilliant Inter Milan, if they don't want him anymore. They must be the best team ever.'

I didn't know a professional footballer could be that good. He was immaculate. Wrighty tells a story about the first night they roomed together. English players tend to lounge about in their boxers on their beds watching telly, scratching themselves. Apparently Dennis came out of the bathroom looking a million dollars in crisp, ironed pyjamas and slippers. That was the style of the man. He was on it all the time, the ultimate professional, there was never any messing about and, although he struggled badly to score in the first half-dozen matches, if you'd seen him in training you just knew it would all click. He'd be out there on his own after we'd all finished, practising his technique, chipping balls from outside the box on to the bar, again and again and again. In the two years we played together we developed a good understanding and he was kind enough to say, 'We've complimented the other's play, we swap around a lot virtually without thinking . . . Paul has a very quick brain and the ability to go with it.' It's taken me a long time not to brush off praise and be embarrassed. Twenty-five years on, I can finally handle it and it feels good.

Bruce changed the way we played. He wanted us to pass more through midfield and we improved from twelfth in the season George was sacked to fifth. Bruce was good for me. He took time at the beginning to have a long walk with me around the training ground and was interested in how I was and where my head was. I could always speak to him and he was straight with me and helpful. Certain people understand you and some never will. Bruce did. You never ask so you don't know if he'd been around addiction before with someone in the family or someone he knew, but he was one of those people who seemed to understand it properly. I played every week, getting back to the top of my game, and if we went away, say, to Sheffield Wednesday on a Friday night, we'd have our dinner and then I could just jump into a cab and go to an AA meeting or whatever I needed. It wasn't a problem. He didn't say, 'None of the other lads are allowed out so I'm not making an exception for you.' He was always very good like that.

Not everyone got on with him so well, and that was his downfall. I had the best treatment from him, but with others he liked to rattle cages, enjoyed a ruck and players steaming into tackles in training. He was also very blunt and kept harking back to his Bolton team. Sometimes you'd wince and think, 'He plays for Arsenal and England, Gaffer, and you're digging him out because you don't think he's as good as one of your old Bolton players. Do me a favour.' It all came to a head with Wrighty. Bruce put him out on the left wing a few times, kept telling him to work harder and seemed to give him a rough ride all the time. Now George was tough but he knew Wrighty responded best to a looser rein – give him a bit of leeway and he would do the business for us. You don't say to Wrighty, 'How did you miss that? John McGinlay would have scored that goal.' You just don't do it. Wrighty was one of the best centre-forwards to have ever played the game.

By the end of the season Bruce was feuding with Wrighty who was now talking about leaving, Tony had been injured, AWOL, off the rails with his drinking and would soon accept that he was an alcoholic, and I wasn't the easiest person to deal with. Still, it felt he'd gone too far when he complained in the dressing room: 'I feel like Marje Proops with you lot.' Saying we were like the women writing in to the *Mirror*'s agony aunt every day wasn't the most tactful approach. Something had to give and, while I was sad to see him go, it wasn't surprising that he was sacked only a week before what should have been the start of his second season. What did shock us was the identity of his successor. Eyebrows and shoulders hit the ceiling at London Colney when vice-chairman David Dein came up to tell us. When he'd gone we all looked at one another – even Dennis – and said, 'Who on earth is Arsène Wenger?'

9

THE ROLLERCOASTER

Because Arsène stayed for twenty-two years and became one of the all-time greats of management, it's easy to forget how exotic his appointment was. He didn't formally take over until the end of September 1996 and when he introduced himself, he instantly became 'Clouseau' as the lads took the piss out of his accent. Ray Parlour kept coming out with lines from the Pink Panther films, but within minutes of him stepping out onto the training pitch and leading his first session, we changed our tune from 'A berm?', 'Your minkey' and 'I am an officeur of the leure' to 'this bloke's a genius'.

First, there was the stretching. On the morning of his first game in charge against Blackburn at Ewood Park, he had us in the hotel ballroom on yoga mats, working every muscle group, arching our backs, freeing our hips. It was gruelling at first and we were all a bit embarrassed; there were as many groans as giggles, but within weeks we all noticed how much more supple and sharp we felt. Then there was the ball work. Out went the days when we'd be 'beasted', nothing but running at London Colney or up and down the Highbury stands until you were sick. Everything was done with the ball. We would do a lot of eight v eight, one-touch routines and then two-touch where the second pass had to go forward or he'd whistle for a free-kick against you. He liked to change the rules to challenge you. Everything was precise, timed to the second on his stop-watch. You had to think quick all the time. There was no 'next goal wins'. Even if we were having a great game, he wouldn't let us go over time. It was so enjoyable. We started turning up earlier and earlier to training, because it was like being at the best school in the world where learning is fun. Not fun as in 'great craic', fun as in you're happy to be there because you can feel yourself getting stronger, better and brighter. I've never been fitter than I was that year.

When the Arsenal lads went away with England they would do Arsène's stretches. The other players would laugh, 'What's that? What the hell are you doing?' In the end, everyone was doing them. He changed our diet: out went all the heavy dishes we'd loved in the past and in came grilled fish in lean portions with rice and loads of green veg. They used to joke about him having shares in broccoli because it came with everything. He banned alcohol from the players' lounge and he brought in supplements and vitamin boosters. We would take Creatine but we wouldn't be left to our own devices to do as he'd asked. It was like clockwork. He wouldn't trust you to do it, just in case you forgot. When we arrived at training, our physio, Gary Lewin, would be there with a cup of orange juice; he'd put in the Creatine, stir it, give it to us to drink while he made sure we did and then we would walk off to get changed. It was like a production line.

There would be caffeine tablets before matches and sugar lumps at half-time to give us an energy hit.

It was a very strong dressing room Arsène walked into, full of senior pros who had won titles and cups and were very set in their ways. But we all bought into it and look what it did for us: Dave Seaman played in the Premier League until he was 40, Lee Dixon 38, Nigel Winterburn 39, Tony Adams 35, Steve Bould 38, Martin Keown 38, Ian Wright 36 and me and Dennis Bergkamp 37.

The other notable thing was Arsène's deep knowledge, long before these things were just a click away, of hundreds of players all across Europe. It brought us Patrick Vieira and Nicolas Anelka in his first season. Patrick was top-class, he covered so much ground, was brilliant in the tackle and a good passer. He was bossing midfields all over the country in only a couple of weeks. Anelka was lethal, razor sharp in front of goal. He had a fantastic career but in those first few days at London Colney I thought he was going to be one of the all-time greats. The two of them cost Wenger £4 million, peanuts even back then.

Off the pitch, I reached two years of sobriety during that season, taking each day at a time. I never thought I could live like that, but one thought kept me going. It was a memory of my last night on drugs when Lorraine tracked me down and reached me on the phone. It was when she told me she had spoken to George Graham and asked me to come home and sort things out. She put my eldest boy Charlie on the line and he said, 'Please come home, Daddy.' But I couldn't put the drink and drugs down. Every day of living well was an attempt to make up for how I had behaved. I did FA campaigns on fitness and on the dangers of gambling, alcohol and drugs. I started to read AA literature and books by addicts in recovery, I read them slowly but I got through them. I spoke to my sponsor and counsellor as well as a lot of people in recovery on the phone and I went to meetings. Some days I would get complacent. I'd think, 'Well, I don't want a drink today, I don't want to have a bet and I certainly don't want to take drugs. I'm all right. I can skip it, I'll watch a film tonight instead of going to a meeting.' It quickly catches up with you, though, and then the depression is suddenly on you again.

I only missed a couple of games that season when I was out after a hernia operation, playing mostly on the right. At the end of it, in the summer of 1997, the club offered me a four-year contract on ten grand a week and I went away on holiday ready to sign it when I came back. I always thought I'd be at Arsenal forever. I couldn't see myself going anywhere else. In the early nineties there were offers from Rangers and I knew that Howard Wilkinson at Leeds had said to George, if you ever sell him, we want him. But he would never sell me, even when I was a total mess. I heard Marcus Rashford say the other day, 'I want to stay at Manchester United for my whole career.' I had a chuckle to myself. I was exactly the same. The problem is, it isn't going to happen. When you get older, it only goes one way if you're not as good as you once were, or you've reached an age when it's a case of cash in now or never. No club is ever going to say he's been loyal to us, so we'll be loyal to him and keep paying him the same sort of money well into his thirties.

When I got back from holiday I didn't have a thought in my brain that I was ever leaving. I was ready to sign the contract but was told that Middlesbrough, who had been relegated from the Premier League in May, had offered £5 million for me. I loved Bryan Robson, Boro's manager, as a player and admired him as a man. He's a legend of the game. Having spoken to him he impressed me even more. He told me that they had just sold Juninho and that he wanted me to lead them back to promotion. He also offered me £20,000 a week. That figure, a million a year, played havoc with my thoughts. I couldn't get it out of my head. I went to speak to Arsène who said, 'I don't want you to go, where can I get a player to replace you for £5 million?' But he also said, when asked why he was leaving it in my court and didn't just reject it: 'Five million is a lot of money for a twenty-nine-year-old.' Arsène came up with an extra two grand a week but wouldn't go any higher, saying Boro, a second tier club, were giving me more than he was paying Dennis and he wouldn't match it. I couldn't get out of my head the difference between what I would earn at Middlesbrough and what I would earn if I stayed. I decided to go and left Arsenal on 99 goals. No disrespect to Boro, I loved my time there. But I do regret it. I did it for the money and that's what you do when you're a gambler. Saying goodbye to my mates wasn't difficult because, however wrong the motive, it had at least been my idea. Whenever I went back, the bonds of affection were still strong and the crowd was always amazing. By a stroke of luck we drew Arsenal in the fourth round of the FA Cup in the January after I left at the Riverside. We lost 2–1 but I got Middlesbrough's goal. I think they let me score in the end and the noise from the travelling support was as loud as the cheers from the Boro fans.

It was the only time I was ever influenced in a career decision by money. When I watched *Match of the Day* with my dad when I was a kid, I didn't know footballers got paid. I played because I loved it, and by the end I didn't even have a contract at my last club, Walsall. When they drew one up I said, 'If you sack me you'll be paying me and it won't be good for the club.' I'd gone completely the other way from 1997 because I knew that money doesn't make you happy. Even though I hadn't had a bet since 1994, I signed for Middlesbrough with a gambler's mindset. A compulsive gambler never thinks, 'Great, I had a win today.' Our first thought is, 'I should have put more on that.' It's a fantasy world, dreaming of lost riches that never existed. I thought that every month that goes by I'd be £35,000 worse off by staying at Arsenal when, of course, I wouldn't be losing anything because I would never have had it in the first place. But to me, the emotions when I thought about the disparity between the two offers were exactly the same as losing a bet without even having the buzz of placing it.

•

One thing you have to learn in recovery is that wherever you go, you have to take your head with you. You sometimes think a change of scenery, 'going geographical' as they say at AA, changes the way you feel. I loved it in North Yorkshire when I got there. It was a fantastic place, the people were amazingly friendly and I played really well. But the truth at the start was that it was the money, Bryan Robson and the challenge he outlined that swung it. When I look back I'm so glad I went. In any case the money all disappeared anyway so it didn't really matter.

I made the decision and thought the family would move up with me. You expect that in football, that it's one of the sacrifices they have to make to follow the main breadwinner around. It's just the way it is. Lorraine had said before, though, that she didn't fancy it. 'We're Londoners,' she said. 'The kids are happy at school. We're settled here and why would you want to drop a division? You've got it good at Arsenal, they've looked after you. You won't get anything better.' And she stuck to her guns. If I was going, I was going on my own. My solution to that problem was to commute. I'd set off at 5 a.m. every morning, driving myself from St Albans to Darlington, M1 on to the M18 and A1. It would take me almost five hours and my back would ache like hell when I got out. I'd train for two hours, long enough to loosen up and shake off the back pain, and then set off back on another five-hour drive and get out of the car with my spine in knots. I only stayed up on the Friday before a match. No wonder I was crap at the start.

After six weeks of that, we'd won four, lost two and drawn two and I had scored only once. Robbo called me in after training and said, 'You've got to move up. Driving is affecting your fitness.' I refused because I knew I would get homesick which could jeopardise my recovery, so we came to a compromise. I would have an extra 90 minutes in bed, drive to Stevenage and get the 7.47 to Newcastle that would arrive in Darlington just after 10 a.m. Boro would lay on a driver to take me to training and when we'd finished I would head back on the 2.01. Training started at 10 o'clock so I was always late but instead of fining me every day I paid for the lads' Christmas party instead. I did that for about another six weeks, but my back was just as bad from sitting on a train for four and a half hours every day. 'Merse, you've got to move up,' Bryan said for the second time and set me up in the house they had rented for Fabrizio Ravanelli in Hutton Rudby. They even gave my brother Keith a job with the club on £400 a week, essentially to keep me company. They treated me brilliantly.

The management team, Robbo, Viv Anderson and Gordon McQueen, were very understanding. You respected them because they'd all been top-drawer players and they knew what it was like. Gordon lived next to us in the village and he and his family could not have been nicer to me. His wife, Yvonne, used to invite us round to dinner along with the other signings and went out of her way to look after us.

Once I moved up we won six and drew one of the next seven. Nigel Pearson was every manager's dream as a captain because he could be Robbo's voice in the dressing room. Sometimes, as a manager you don't want to keep coming in and making the players listen to the same old words, moaning about this and that. But if the captain can tear into players while they're getting changed before the manager talks, it's a massive help. If you weren't pulling your weight, Nigel would tell you. No doubt about it. He was up there with Tony Adams as the best captain I played under. He wasn't scared of confronting players even if he wasn't having a good game himself. He would never hide. If he was having a bad game, he still gave his all. If someone else wasn't working their socks off, he would dig them out. When you've got a captain like that, you're halfway there as a manager.

You can tell how well it went by the number of games I played – 45 out of 46, scoring 12 goals and being named in the PFA Championship team of the year. We beat Liverpool over two legs in a League Cup semi-final. We were a Championship side and we beat a team of Liverpool's magnitude, a team that would finish third in the Premier League, over two legs. Sometimes you can win against a majorly more talented team over 90 minutes but it is very rare that you defeat that quality of player over two legs. We played Chelsea in the final in a hard game which we only lost in extra time, but it was a step too far. Beating Liverpool was the highlight of my time at Middlesbrough; to do that over two legs and for me to score in both games was a reminder that even though I had dropped out of the Premier League I was still good enough.

Bryan was a far better manager than his reputation would suggest. He put a really good team together with leaders in Nigel Pearson and Andy Townsend and also strengthened at exactly the right time. I played with Mikkel Beck, a proper, hard-working striker who scored 14 goals, but just when we needed a lift he brought in Marco Branca from Inter Milan who was thirty-three but still a class act. He bagged nine in 11 games. Bryan called me in towards the end of the season when we had lost to Sheffield United 1–0 at Bramall Lane and I'd missed a penalty. There were six games to go and we were third. Nottingham Forest were miles ahead, Sunderland were four points above us and had Niall Quinn and Kevin Phillips on fire up front. They weren't losing and it didn't look like they were going to slip up, and Robbo said, 'You're tired. Go on holiday for two weeks, refresh yourself and get ready for the play-offs.' I refused. 'No, we've got a chance,' I said. 'They've only got to lose one game and then we're in.' We won five and drew one of the last six and Sunderland drew at home with QPR who were in the bottom four, and lost at Ipswich. We went up by one point and although I didn't go on holiday, I won't forget how thoughtful Bryan was, trying to look after me as well as the best interests of the club. The top managers always knew how to get the best out of me.

•

As well as Marco Branca, Robbo signed Paul Gascoigne for the run-in and he came to live with me and my brother in the Ravanelli house. If ever I was going to relapse you would think it would be provoked by living with a fellow alcoholic (not that he recognised he was an addict at the time). In truth, though, I started gambling again a month before Gazza joined us from Rangers. In the past, when I've looked back I would blame the stress of the promotion campaign, of being given a mission and feeling huge responsibility for pulling it off. Add in the loneliness and isolation of being 220 miles from home, plus having the hump with Lorraine for not moving up and her having the hump with me for not being around, and you would think it was a disaster waiting to happen. 'Boredom', I always used to say, was another reason I began betting again, starting with £50 stakes on the horses in February and ending with £100 punts in April, by which time I'd blown seven grand. People would say, 'Well, what do you expect? He finishes work at 1 p.m. and sits around all day doing nothing.' It's not true. It's not that footballers have too much opportunity to bet. Dennis Bergkamp never went home and gambled. Ian Wright didn't finish training and do all his money. It's not boredom, it's because I couldn't cope with life as it was and needed to escape. You have to be able to live life on life's terms, deal with all the strains and how they make you feel. And when you can't do that, a compulsive gambler will choose to gamble. It doesn't matter if you've got empty hour after empty hour or you're as busy as anything, you gamble. Boredom does not feed the compulsion, the illness. It's life and the inability to cope with the way it makes you feel that drives relapses and you fall back into the welcoming arms of an old, familiar 'friend'. The compulsion overwhelms all reason.

It was missing meetings that triggered my first bets for more than three years. Addiction loves having you to itself, thrives on you being alone and hates it when you're around good people. The illness doesn't want you going to meetings, talking to people in recovery, it wants you in a room on your own, knowing that sooner or later you'll have a bet or a drink again. You hear it all the time at GA and AA: 'I have to keep coming, I have to keep talking to people because my addiction's out there waiting to mug me.' As night follows day, I started drinking again, too. Not in the old way but indoors with Gazza and, typically with him, it wasn't straightforward. We lived in a really quiet village in the middle of nowhere. It was a goldfish bowl existence, the pubs were off limits because everyone would know your business if you went out so we would sit in the house and play this mad game, me, Keith, Gazza and Jimmy Five Bellies. It was a game we made up for a laugh. I say it was harmless and luckily enough it was in the end, but looking back now it could have killed one of us. Gazza was hooked on sleeping tablets. He thought if he slept most of the day he couldn't eat and put on weight. He invented this game where he would deal them out to the four of us. We'd all put a lump of cash in the middle and take a pill with every glass of red wine we'd knock back. Glass of wine . . . pill . . . another glass . . . another pill. The object of the game was not to fall asleep and whoever stayed up longest won the pot. After a couple of hours, you might think you'd won and go to grab the cash, only for someone to stir and you'd have to have more wine and a tablet. My brother usually won. In some ways it wasn't that bad. We'd be in bed fast asleep at 8 p.m., it's not as if we were in a Newcastle nightclub until four in the morning.

Gazza is the nicest bloke you could wish to meet. Life was lived at 100 miles an hour but that used to be the way I wanted it. I always searched for that rollercoaster. That's been my problem. You play football and you're on the biggest adrenaline ride ever, it's the ultimate. You score a goal and there's nothing better. There's no larger buzz than that. But when you come off, normal people can go home and unwind. I wanted to stay up there. I was comfortable around him and his antics. The wildness suited me. It was hectic, one minute up, one minute down. He would never wear any clothes round the house and, despite us having six bedrooms, he would always kip on the sofa, which added to that sense of an unreal existence. That was the place where the craziness happened and I kept a lid on it outside. My God, though, we laughed so much. One day, he rang Paul Walsh and told him he was pulling out of his testimonial the following day unless he agreed that my brother could play. Keith wasn't bothered about playing but Gazza thought it would be a brilliant moment for him, something to remember for the rest of his life. Walshie reluctantly agreed and Keith, a van driver not a footballer, went all the way down to Portsmouth from Middlesbrough as Gazza's guest, played in the match and scored. Gazza was always up to something, trying to make people laugh, trying to make people's days. What I look for now, that steady life, could not have been more different to those three months.

•

When I went into treatment in 1994 and started on the twelve-step programme, my counsellors said you've got to have a goal. Without a moment's hesitation, I said it was to play for England again and they went, 'Woah, woah! Aim a bit lower than that.' Their worry was that it had to be achievable and, because Terry Venables had said he would never pick me, that failing to earn a recall would be a crushing blow. But Terry left after Euro '96, Glenn Hoddle got the job and he liked me, picking me in my last months at Arsenal for the qualifier at Wembley against Italy. I think he could see a bit of him in me. 'You see the picture,' he told me. I knew that when I left Arsenal and became a Championship player, I'd probably ruined my chances of going to the 1998 World Cup. He picked me for a couple of B-internationals in the spring of 1998 and made me captain. I gave it everything and I played very well. 'Still,' I thought, 'who goes to the World Cup from the league I'm in?'

I did. To go to the World Cup when you're not playing in the Premier League is a massive achievement, I realise now, and I owe it all to Glenn. I remember Ray Parlour saying to me after he'd just won the Double at Arsenal in 1998 and wasn't getting a look-in with England, that Arsène rang Glenn to ask why. They knew each other from their time at

Monaco together and he told Glenn that Ray was playing superbly, made a vital contribution to winning the Double and that he did not understand why he wasn't involved. He turned to Ray after he put the phone down and said, 'You've just got to hope he gets the sack.' When Kevin Keegan came in, Ray played for England but I never got a call-up. Ray was no better in 2000 than he was in 1998, I was better in 2000 than I was two years earlier. It's all about the manager. If he likes you, you've got a chance. If not . . . you're stuffed.

Ray having a laugh with the lads about what he claimed to have said when he went to see Glenn's faith healer Eileen Drewery – 'short back and sides, please, Eileen' – didn't help. I went to Eileen with an open mind and liked her. I was struggling so badly with the gambling relapse, bottling it up and keeping it secret out of shame, that I would try anything. It had sent me into a deep depression, but I didn't know that's what it was. I'd be so down that I couldn't get out of bed and the paranoia, which had never really gone away, ramped up. It seemed that everybody was looking at me, judging me. I thought, 'I need something to work here.' And whatever help was offered, I would try it. Eileen gave me that calmness, settled my raging doubts and was a big part of me being in the right frame of mind to go out to La Manga with the squad of twenty-eight, which was to be cut to twenty-two after the warm-up games.

It was an odd week. Too many of us felt on trial and I was convinced I'd be one of the six who wouldn't make it to the World Cup. I don't know why Glenn did it that way, it was unsettling and there was an air of tension. I expect Glenn thought it would keep everyone on their toes, but most players were a bag of nerves. He wasn't the best man-manager, at times he became impatient when a player couldn't do what he wanted. Because he could still play, he often joined in and demonstrated something by doing it himself. After a while players get frustrated with that, a bit jealous. If he had been better at handling people and hadn't said all that weird stuff about disabled people and karma, he would still be England manager now. No one could touch him as a tactician.

We flew back and forth to Casablanca twice to play the warm-up matches and I started the second one, a 0–0 draw with Belgium. I thought I played well but hadn't done enough to swing it. We were due to be told on the Sunday and the night before, as a reward for the hard week's work, we were allowed to have a few drinks. Big mistake. Not for me, I spent the evening with Tony Adams in the coffee shop, but Gazza got pissed, followed it up the next day by drinking on the golf course while we waited for Glenn's verdict, and the two recovering alcoholics had to throw him in the pool to try to sober him up before he sat down with the manager.

It didn't work. He'd been all over the papers before we flew out, flashbulbs going off in his face after lengthy sessions with his mates, Chris Evans and Danny Baker. Now this. The fact that he'd carried on drinking into Sunday was his downfall. I had said jokingly during the week that once Glenn told me I wouldn't be going to the World Cup, I'd kick off and trash his room. Gazza always blamed me for putting the idea in his head. As soon as Glenn let him know that he was out of the squad in his one-to-one, he turned into Keith Moon and started smashing up the furniture. He was in a terrible state when I caught up with him in his own room, bleeding, crying, not making much sense. It was awful to see him like that. Having lived with him for three months, though, and seen how he was drinking, I knew he was in a bad place.

My turn to see Glenn came towards the end of his twenty-eight meetings and he told me I was in. 'I hope I'm not going just because he isn't,' I said. 'No,' said Glenn. 'You were both on that plane.' I think Gazza had just pushed him too far since playing so well in the draw with Italy that got us to the World Cup. He must have thought: 'If he's like that after a week, what's he going to do when he's locked up with us for six weeks?'

Being cooped up at a sealed World Cup training base is enough to fray anyone's nerves, let alone someone in Gazza's near crisis state. The tournament itself was hard. There were a few of us who never looked like getting a chance, and it was very frustrating. If Glenn had taken Gazza to use as an impact sub as he had planned, not as a sure starter for every game in France's midsummer heat, he would probably have ended up more restless than even we were. You want to stay upbeat and supportive of the lads, make sure they do well. But the ones who aren't playing will start messing about because we would be on our own for long spells of training. We'd be running out with 'Valderrama', 'Dunga' or

'Hagi' written on our backs just to lighten the mood. Around the hotel I hung around with Tony and Michael Owen a lot, playing golf, pool, snooker and table tennis, anything to get away from the temptation to bet.

There's being sober and there's being dry. If you're a dry drunk and not doing the meetings there isn't any difference. You're just not drinking. You're still going to be selfish, still have a short fuse, everything's going to irritate you. For a dry drunk, it's all right saying I haven't had a drink for six months, but if you haven't changed, if you're not a better person, what's the point? There are some days now when my wife, Kate, will say, 'You need a meeting.' And I will because I've got back to how I was when I was gambling and drinking, moody and ratty, but I'm not boozing or betting. That's the difference between being dry and sobriety. You have to change. It's just the same with gambling. At the World Cup, the urge to have a bet, though I was resisting it, was there most of the time and my mind turned back to the way it had been before, down and anxious. Glenn was like Arsène (apart from that one mistake in Spain) in that no drink was allowed, so booze-wise it was easy. But everyone was punting on the first goalscorer, betting on the games because they were all live, and we had private bookmakers in the squad, Alan Shearer and Teddy Sheringham. I felt surrounded by it. I didn't gamble yet I couldn't shake those thoughts dominating my head. It was back to white-knuckling it again. I fended those thoughts off with constant activity, in fierce competition with young Michael on the pool table and talking to Tony. Having another alcoholic around, someone I'd known since we were kids, was a big help because he understood the struggles when the urge is on you but also because, as the person who led the way, I didn't want my relapse to affect his recovery.

I didn't feature in any of the group games and I never thought I'd get on in the last 16 match against Argentina. But when David Beckham was unjustly sent off for lashing out at Diego Simeone, I was suddenly in the frame and went on with 15 minutes to go. It was a great game, really tight even though it was 10 v 11, and full of quality. Despite the drama of Sol Campbell 'scoring', we ended extra-time at 2–2 and we gathered in the centre-circle to work out the order for the penalty shootout. Glenn announced it was Alan, Paul Ince, Michael, me and David Batty. The last time I'd taken a penalty was at Bramall Lane when the goal shrank before my eyes and it was saved. I was usually reliable from the spot, but I was panicking like crazy when he named me.

A couple of weeks earlier we'd hit some turbulence before we landed in Casablanca for one of those friendlies. I'm a very nervous flyer. Even now, although I've flown hundreds of times all over the world, I've been known to cancel trips on the morning of the flight because I can't face it. It depends where my head is on any given day. As we descended through the Atlas mountains, I was sweating, bricking it and groaning. Glenn was in front of me and turned to speak: 'Don't worry Merse, it's okay. We're not going to crash.' He has an aura about him, really soothing, an inner serenity that oozes belief and that he's in control. Just him saying those words and the way he said them, calmed me down.

He was the same that night in Saint-Etienne. I was thinking, what if I do a Stuart Pearce or Chris Waddle or Gareth Southgate and let down my wife, my kids, my mum and dad and my country? Glenn put his hand on my chest, stared into my eyes and said, very deliberately. 'You. Will. Not. Miss.' I trusted Glenn so much I believed him. All the butterflies, all the nausea left me. I knew I would score and even though their goalkeeper, Carlos Roa, tried to mess with me by arguing with the referee over the placement of the ball, the goal was as big as a house. I couldn't miss. The keeper went the right way but he was never going to stop it. Seconds later, David Batty joined Incey in missing and we were out. No one would have taken being the one to miss better than David. He was the ultimate player for having the right perspective: 'I got up, I took it, I missed. Move on.'

It was another one of those nearly situations in my England career. Who is to say I wouldn't have played in the quarter-final? We defended well with me on against Argentina, and Beckham would have been suspended if we had gone through to play Holland. I take one of the pens and score and maybe it could have been a different game and tournament then.

The World Cup for me could have been like my 1999–2000 season at Aston Villa when I wasn't in the team until December yet ended up as player of the year. It could have been a slow start but a big finish. We didn't make it far enough to find out. It's very rare that you get knocked out in the last 16 and come back as heroes. All anyone expects of you is to give everything you've got – that's because all the people back home, even though they can't play, would assure you that if they played for England they would give their all. They love people working hard because that's what they would do if they were in the team and they appreciated us for doing that and coming so close. That's why they weren't waiting for us at Luton Airport with the rotten tomatoes.

They were waiting for David Beckham with something worse, trying to make out he was a villain, and some idiot hanged an effigy of him from a lamp-post. It wasn't his fault. I don't blame him at all. It was a yellow card at worst, but the way the tabloids went for him was cruel and off the scale. I experienced some of that public notoriety, but I never had the whole country against me. I had my demons working against me as well as my critics – even so it was like nothing compared with the hate thrown at David. I don't think people give him enough respect. To come back and have the career he had and be the good person he is, not many could have done that, especially in those days when the view was 'Get on with it' and you didn't get the protection from the club and the FA that they provide now. If it happened in 2021, it would rightly be seen as scandalous. Actually, it was scandalous back then.

Three and a half years after leaving rehab, I had not only achieved my goal of playing for England again, I'd also

scored a penalty in the most stressful circumstances imaginable. I've always needed something to strive for, a target to
drive me. Instead of sitting back in satisfaction, I thought,
'Shit, what do I do now?' I didn't really replace that goal with
another one and not long after coming home the wheels fell
off again.

10

SOBRIETY

I had managed to hold it together in France. The World Cup is a powerful distraction, but the dark moods that had been haunting me since February were now at the front of my mind. Out of the England bubble, within a few hours I felt like I had crashed. We went away on holiday to Portugal with another family and I found it hard to relax or even relate to the adults in the state I was in, brooding about betting, hating myself for thinking about it so much. I was constantly restless. I hung out with the kids instead, trying to occupy myself that way, in the pool, playing games.

I'd bought a house on the Wynyard estate near Stockton-on-Tees in the spring as a family home for us and also as an escape from 'the madhouse' in Hutton Rudby which we were due to move into at the start of the season. Lorraine helped choose the house, liked it and had agreed to come up with the children. But when we got home after Portugal there were delays and arguments. She said she didn't want to move while I was so depressed and snappy. They did come up briefly to join me, though by that point I had realised that I had to get out of Middlesbrough. The marriage, even if I didn't recognise it at the time, was coming to an end as well.

When we got back from holiday, I took my eldest son Charlie and a friend of his up to the new house for a few days for the pre-season friendlies. As soon as I was up north, I withdrew £10,000 from the bank, stuck £4,000 of it on a Scottish football accumulator and lost it. Next day I lumped on Dewsbury, a second-tier rugby league team, to win a match against Leigh by 20 points. They were too obscure for regular Teletext updates so I took to ringing up the lady on the club's switchboard for the score every few minutes. They were 20 points up at half-time but the opposition fought back and gradually whittled the lead down. It was 26–18 at the final whistle but I had already slammed the phone down on her for the final time by then, ending a sequence of increasingly agitated calls with 'What a load of crap your team is.' I pulled myself back from the brink for a few days, but after I'd taken the boys home to St Albans, I was on my own, rattling round a big, empty house, antsy and with nothing and no one to restrain me. I was off the leash.

I joined Gazza and Chris Waddle and some mates of theirs on a charity golf day and when Gazza offered me a swig from a bottle of schnapps he had stashed in his golf bag, I took it. There was a rage that came over me that had been brewing for months and the booze was like a release valve. The red wine and sleeping pills game had brought me back to drinking but it wasn't drinking in the old way, it was like an add-on to the tablets, something to strengthen the cosh on your head that sent you to sleep. The schnapps was the start of a session, my first for almost four years, which led to shandy, lager, Guinness and vodka-Red Bulls on the Quayside in Newcastle. That night it lightened my mood and brought me out of my shell, but in the morning I was full of fear and shame.

The relapse was inevitable for me once I'd stopped going to meetings. I would get it into my head that a new group wasn't for me, or I couldn't face sitting for an hour with people who smoked all the time, or I was too busy. I couldn't see that the addicts who go regularly to meetings are a mutual preservation society. People who haven't had a drink or a bet for thirty years need meetings and those who haven't had a bet for a couple of days need those thirty-year veterans at the meetings. A thirty-year clean and sober person needs a newcomer to tell him how bad it is and the newcomer needs the sober veteran not only to tell him it can be done but mainly to show him. They're the proof that it's possible. The meetings are the medicine. If you're ill, you get medicine from the doctor. And it's the same with this. When I am not going to meetings my head goes haywire, I stop getting well, just as I would if I was physically sick and stopped the medication before I was cured. With addiction, the cure is never finished. For me it's a lifelong job.

If anyone asks me how to get clean and sober, I always say, 'Go to a meeting.' It's impossible for me to stay sober without them. Believe me, I've tried. It's rare but some people can do it another way. My dad, for instance, stopped drinking without the meetings. He just got up one morning about five years ago and decided to stop. He drank, really drank, then one day he just said, 'I can't do this anymore' and gave up. I thought there was no way he could do it but he has been absolutely unbelievable. Not everybody is wired like that. I'm not. There are a few things that helped him – he is getting on now, he's only around my mum and brother, doesn't get out much and he is not out on the high streets where drinking goes on 24/7. He can steer well clear. I'm not around it anymore, but those last weeks at Middlesbrough I saw it everywhere.

In the Boro squad I could see people enjoying themselves, doing what I'd been up to six or seven years before. Selfishly, I couldn't handle it. I shouldn't have been so judgemental because when I was doing it, I thought it was great. I was full of self-pity: 'Poor me. Poor Paul. If I can't do it anymore then they need to stop or I need to leave.' Those thoughts tell you that my recovery wasn't good and robust. I can sit around people having a drink or a bet now, but back then I couldn't stand them being able to bring the *Racing Post* in when I couldn't, or talk about Tuesday nights out and what they got up to on Saturdays when I couldn't. Looking back now, I'd stopped drinking but hadn't fundamentally changed and the old feelings came back when I was on my own: 'Poor Paul can't do that.' I wouldn't want to go back to that life now in a million years. After the World Cup, at my lowest, I envied everyone their consequence-free enjoyment of the things I could no longer do.

I told Bryan Robson that I'd had a night out on the drink and that I wanted to go back into treatment. He asked me to give it some time, to see if it was just a one-off, and we went away on a short tour of the Netherlands. Although I didn't drink out there, my head was all over the place and I couldn't bottle up all the anger and resentment. I could feel four years' of abstinence, four years of hard work invested in the recovery, evaporating into thin air. While I always tracked back as a player to do my defensive job, I would never steam into a tackle. In the first match against Heerenveen, I got sent off for a late, reckless foul. All of a sudden, I had this desire to chin the referee. It was insane. Thank God I managed to walk away but I ripped off my shirt, chucked it at our bench and sat in the dressing room on my own, stewing. 'This isn't me,' I thought. I was genuinely terrified of the fury I was feeling. I calmed down enough to go out with the lads that night, stuck to Diet Coke and, because I was now suspended for the second game, flew home early the next day. That evening Lorraine wouldn't let me into the house. I don't think she knew I had relapsed with drink but we had been arguing relentlessly and she was fed up with me. I went to the Noke Hotel, booked in, ordered a vodka and orange, called a mate and went out on another long, long session.

I was scared to death when I woke up the following morning. I didn't want to drink my recovery away. I didn't want to gamble my life away. I needed help and knew the only way back was through AA and GA. I asked my mate to go home and pick up my books. As soon as I started reading the literature and going back to meetings, the anger started to lift. I still wanted to leave Boro, though. I felt if I stayed there, through no fault of the players and the club, I'd have been back into my old habits again full-time. I wanted to get back south, because my wife wouldn't move up. As I've said, though, it doesn't matter where you go, you take your head with you. Bryan wouldn't let me leave at first and I played the first three games of the season, losing one and drawing two. That added to my frustration – I thought we were going to get beaten most weeks and I hate losing.

George Graham used to have this saying whenever you would ask for more money than he wanted to pay you. 'You might think the grass is greener elsewhere,' he would say. 'But just walk away from here and you'll see nothing matches up to Arsenal.' I got the nickname Vic, after Victor Meldrew, at Boro, because I complained so much. Later at Villa, John Gregory would say to me, 'No matter what we do, it isn't going to be good enough for you, is it Merse?' And even Harry Redknapp said that I needed careful handling on the training ground, 'Paul would always be moaning about something. If it was two-touch he'd want to play all-in. If it was all-in, he'd want to play two-touch.'

George was right, you see. Arsenal is a Rolls Royce of a club. It just oozed class from the marble halls, the Art Deco dressing rooms at Highbury, immaculate training ground, the rigour of George's routines and the brilliance of the sessions Arsène put on. It was so much more professional compared with my other clubs. Everything was done with a bit of style and attention to detail. It's an eye-opener once you've left when things at other training grounds don't match up and that's what I was trying to get across. The lads used to laugh at me, but I think my moaning helped by sending out a message that my attitude was 'I'm here to win. I'm not here to mess about.' And if we were not winning, no one would have the hump more than me. If we were playing a practice match with little goals, it would annoy me. 'What are we playing with little goals for? We play with big goals on a Saturday, so what's the point of having little goals?' I'd always have a moan but I'd always work. It comes with experience. The older you get the more you moan. When you've got hundreds of games under your belt, you've been around for years, you've done enough training sessions to know when it's good or bad.

I never minded being called Victor Meldrew, 'high maintenance' and 'a right pain in the arse', but I was impressed with the way Bryan treated me. For someone who was a legend in the game, he must have found me frustrating. If I didn't think it was right I refused to do stuff in training, or I would get angry about a routine or a bleep test or something, yet instead of him saying, 'I'll show him who's the boss in front of everyone else', he would pull me aside for a quiet chat and let me do what was best for me. It was never about his ego. He could easily have gone the other way. He could have thought, 'Who do you fucking think you are? I'm Bryan Robson, I'm one of the greatest midfield players who ever lived. I trained like that so you train like that.' But he didn't.

He was clever. His only thoughts were, 'I need to get the best out of this player. When he plays well we've got more of a chance.' He understood I had problems, needed help and tried to make me as happy as I could be. 'Let him get on with it, we'll ride with it' was his approach and because of it I managed to help deliver promotion as he had asked.

In the end he agreed to sell me, angered when someone stitched me up by telling the papers there was a booze and gambling culture at the club. One paper reported that I was telling people my recovery was in jeopardy and I blamed the bad influences in the dressing room. It was a complete distortion of what I'd actually said, which was that it wasn't really about what was going on around me. It was about what was going on inside my head. Gazza was pissed off with me, too, until I rang him to let him know it hadn't been down to me but someone I foolishly trusted. Because of that story I left under a shadow, which disappoints me. Everyone loves Juninho; he was with them a season, played well, got relegated and went off to Spain. I left one of the best clubs in Europe to play in the Championship, I was with them a season, played well, helped get them promoted and left but my departure enraged a lot of people and that outrage was hurtful. I had done my job. Of course, there was a lot less understanding about addiction in 1998. In those days I wasn't 'ill', I was 'weak and greedy'. It hurt me because I loved Middlesbrough but my marriage was about to crack, my recovery had wobbled too many times for comfort and I was desperate to be around my kids. It really was as simple as that.

Tottenham's offer was the one Middlesbrough wanted to accept. Having priced me at £6.75 million at the age of thirty, Boro would have taken Chris Armstrong plus £4 million in cash from Spurs. The only problem was I wouldn't have gone to Tottenham for £100,000 a week. They were wasting their time. I had too much respect for Arsenal fans. Supporters *are* football. They make every club what it is. I don't care who you are, how big a player you are, the game is about the fans. And I wouldn't have signed for Birmingham when I left Villa or Southampton after playing for Portsmouth, or Newcastle or Sunderland after Middlesbrough for that matter. It's why I have maintained a good rapport with a lot of the fans of those clubs. I'm a Chelsea fan but love each club I played for and understand the supporters' code. I hope they know I would never cross the divide between one of my clubs and their bitterest rivals. No chance.

It was Andy Townsend, my team-mate at Middlesbrough and a former captain of Aston Villa, who alerted me to their interest. He was a great bloke, Andy, a terrific player, one of the funniest men in football I've ever met. He knew Villa inside-out and still had strong connections there. One day early in the season, after Villa had sold Dwight Yorke to Manchester United and it was known in the game that they were going to spend the £12 million they'd received, he said to me, 'Villa are interested in you. Do you fancy it?' I said, 'Wow, yeah. Definitely.' They had some very good players, they were top of the league and, crucially, it was 150 miles closer to St Albans. Once they knew I was interested, they put the bid in. In the Premier League, it's already done before it's done. When a player is transferred, the agent's sorted it all out, the fee and the wages, long before it's made public. You don't go to a club and say 'I want to leave' and then they go, 'Of course you can leave.' You don't go home and think, 'Hmm. Who should I go to next, given there's no club after me yet?' It's all settled beforehand. Bryan was upset and rightly so because he was losing a good player for his club, but we patched it up after only a couple of days and we've been good friends ever since.

A month later, I was asked to go to the Priory at Roehampton to talk to Gazza, who was at the clinic after a terrible couple of episodes of heavy drinking that had been splashed all over the newspapers and generated genuine concern for his safety. I went down to see him after an England game, expecting to talk to him about my experiences; how, after that relapse with him that began on the golf course, I was now back in recovery, taking one day at a time, with no goal other than not having a drink or a bet today. We spoke for a while but he was very jittery, one moment talking about wanting to get well, next minute about doing a bunk. When the nurse rang to ask me to come in, she mentioned that rock legend Eric Clapton, a volunteer helper there, had asked to see us both and he joined us in Gazza's room. He was very gracious, very humble. After talking for a while, telling us the story of his recovery, giving advice and practical help, he offered to go and fetch us some coffee. As soon as he left,

Gazza sat up and said, 'Who the fuck's that tramp?' Typically, he didn't have a clue about much beyond football.

I always thought that when Gazza said after many bouts of treatment that he would never drink or take drugs again, it was a hostage to fortune. Forever is a long, long time. It's daunting. But if you break it down to just today, it's doable. We can all be world record holders in not having a drink for one day. And then try to do it again tomorrow. I would never judge Gazza, who remains the loveliest bloke. I interviewed him one-on-one on Sky a couple of years ago and it was a delight. He has been interviewed a million times but if you watch our one, you will see he is so warm and relaxed and just talks naturally. In most interviews, because he has been burned so many times, he is cautious in what he says. That day he was comfortable around me and spoke candidly. I'll always treasure his friendship. I just hope the penny drops one day and he thinks, 'I've had enough of this.' That's the feeling that saved me after so many relapses. I finally reached a place where I just had enough of feeling the way I did all the time. Only when he gets to that point will he find a way to negotiate this horrible disease.

•

Aston Villa was a fantastic move for me. I was getting older and appreciated football at thirty 100 times more than I did when I was twenty. Villa saw the best of me. At thirty-two,

I was better than I was at twenty-two. When you're twenty you don't think it's ever going to end. I won the league at twenty-one and twenty-three and you think you're going to be thereabouts at the top all the time, but you're not. These opportunities are rare and you have to take advantage when you can. In life too many people worry about what they're going to do tomorrow or what they did yesterday and piss on today. Today just goes. You have to live your life in the moment. Look at Michael Jordan in *The Last Dance*. No one lives in the moment more than him – the past is irrelevant, the future does not exist, all that counts is now.

For a lot of my time at Villa, after a sticky start, because I was well and going to meetings, I got to that place, too. I played the best football of my whole career. I won everything at Arsenal and won nothing at Villa but I was consistently a far better player at Villa than I had been when regularly winning medals and awards. When you're older, you know the game better and you know life better. Towards the end of my time at Arsenal I was asked to go on an ITV documentary called *Peak Performance* that monitored my brain activity as I scanned the pitch while playing, reading the game. It found that I had an unusual ability to process space and positions almost instantaneously which allowed me to identify more options than most players. At my best in my thirties, it was like having second sight. I look at Jamie Vardy – he's a better footballer at thirty-four than he was five years ago. I admire him so much for what he's achieved and his determination to stay there. The best footballers will tell you it's easy to get to the top because you have that drive, it's 'me against them' and when you come from non-league like Vardy, or me, a tiny kid who can't get a game in the youth team, there's an end goal. To have that desire to kick on again once you've got there, that's what makes the special players.

I know the Villa chairman at the time, the late Sir Doug Ellis, was not popular with the fans at various points during his long ownership but he was brilliant with me. He loved players with a bit of swagger and when I moved to the area we ended up as neighbours. I'd often pop over the road for a cup of tea and a chat. He treated me like one of his sons, absolutely loved me and loved the club. I never left his company without feeling he valued me as a man as much as a footballer and wanted the best for me. That's not how relationships with chairmen usually are. With Doug there was a genuine warmth.

That wasn't the case at first with John Gregory. We continued our unbeaten run from the start of the season to a club record 12 games and although I was struggling with a sore back I was annoyed to be substituted so frequently towards the end of games when I thought I was playing well. I started to question why he had signed me and wondered if it had been more the chairman than John behind it. He was quite remote at first, as we sussed each other out, and bridges had to be built when he felt my criticisms went too far – like the time he insisted the players had a team photo on the pitch after that 12th game, a 4–1 victory over Southampton, when we were top of the league. I thought it was too flash, embarrassing, acting like we'd already won something, and I had a pop. I hid at the back but shouted, 'We won the Double? Is the Premiership trophy and FA Cup down there at the front?' The response, predictably, was 'Shut up, Merse.'

The back pain started because I was commuting again. This time it took only 75 minutes and I now had a driver but I was still feeling stiff when I arrived at Villa's Bodymoor Heath training ground. I stayed at the Belfry before matches and went home on Saturday night, having moved back into the house following the transfer from Middlesbrough, which had been well received at home. John had this habit, though, of insisting we turn in on Sunday mornings. The first time he did it, I couldn't believe it because when I got there all he wanted us to do was have a long soak in the bath. I went mad. 'It takes two and a half hours to get here and back . . . for a fucking bath?' I fumed. 'Yeah,' he said. 'Your contract says you have to live within 20 minutes' drive of Villa Park. You're meant to be living up here.' Fair enough, there was no answer to that except I think it was snide, a power play. My recovery was based in London. I stayed there because my family, my meetings and network were there and all three were crucial to me being well. We were at loggerheads for some time, clashing over tactics and selection. It wasn't working out. I thought it was only fair that I tried a different approach.

I wasn't easy to live with as an addict or in the first years of sobriety. I became a good father again after rehab but sometimes I was very hard work as a partner, sometimes crabby, sometimes tearful, a slave to my dark moods. I always used to say I was a good dad and a shit husband. I've realised subsequently that I was still sick. So try as we might, we just weren't getting on at home. Lorraine and I separated, which forced me, before the divorce, to move out and up to Sutton Coldfield at the end of my first season with Villa. John sort of met me halfway to mend our relationship, giving me time to talk and explain myself. And from then on we got on great.

Before those happier days, however, there was the biggest bust-up of the lot. The back pain became chronic in November and eventually I was diagnosed with a herniated disc. I missed six weeks' football and went round the houses looking for help, having an epidural and then stretching and massage. Between Christmas and New Year I started gambling again, losing about ten grand on assorted football bets over three days by getting a mate to stick them on for me. My mind was a blur and it was as if I was on autopilot, glued to the telly and early internet sites for the American football scores, on the phone to my friend until he reached the credit limit on his bookies' account and I had to stop. I felt bad, as I always did, but more forgiving of myself this time, knowing how low I felt without football, the pain and uncertainty of a bad back worse than the relative simplicity of a muscle or bone injury with a fixed return date. I got lonely without the camaraderie of the dressing room and, because I couldn't train, had all this nervous energy I couldn't run off. I was going in most days to do my stretches and would go to the games but I felt like an intruder. One weekend in January, I hatched a plan to fly with my brother and a mate to watch New York Jets play Jacksonville Jaguars in the NFL play-offs to shake me out of the gloom. I asked for the weekend and Monday off to rest my back, which was granted. After training on the Friday, I flew to JFK on Concorde. To get tickets from the NFL office in London, I had agreed to do some interviews at Meadowlands, so how I thought I'd get away with it is beyond me now. The trip was costing ten grand so I rang my mate back home to put eleven grand on the Jets to win at 10–11 to pay for the weekend. That bet actually came in, thank God, or I would have been looking at a £21,000 weekend instead of one that seemingly cost nothing.

It didn't take long for the papers to find out. John Gregory was obviously not happy and he cold-shouldered me for a couple of days, filtering criticism out onto the back pages about plane seats not being very good for longstanding back injuries. I had my say after playing a reserve game when interviewed by Sky, saying the addictions were part of the package with me and that I had felt very down and needed the lift of that trip. I hadn't lied, I just hadn't told them what I was doing with my weekend off and if they weren't prepared to be understanding, I would leave.

It could have escalated even more but it was then that we both took a deep breath, I met the manager and we had a long, clear-the-air chat. He fined me two weeks' wages for not letting him know where I was going – that 'freebie' now cost £50,000 – but from then on we got on brilliantly because he started to understand how I ticked. I apologised, explained what it was like when I went stir crazy and how he could trust me to know the right way to manage my addictions, which would make me the best player I could be for his football club. From that point on he was as good as gold with me, eventually making me captain. I played really well and scored some spectacular goals. I was named Villa player of the tear twice in four seasons, but would have loved to win something. We came close, runners-up in the FA Cup, League Cup semi-finalists and had a couple of long spells at the top of the league before fading away to sixth, sixth, eighth and eighth. Villa had some very good players in the £4 million to £7 million bracket but not the extra quality that Manchester United, Arsenal and Chelsea were buying in the £10 million to £15 million class. That's the difference between titles and cups and no cigars.

It was a very good dressing room and after those first few months I always felt I could talk to the lads about how I was feeling. You could tell people around the table how you were and they listened and were interested. This was a long time ago, before there was a broader awareness in society, never mind football, of mental health issues. They were always very supportive of me: Ugo Ehiogu, God rest his soul, Mark Bosnich, Gareth Southgate, Ian Taylor and Dion Dublin were big players, real good men, wonderful team-mates.

How Ian never played for England I will never know. He was box-to-box, scored goals and made goals. We expected central midfielders to get up and down in those days and he was one of the best. Gareth Barry came through at seventeen and no one mentions him when we talk about the Premier League greats, but twenty years later he was still playing at the highest level. How many kids are first-team regulars at a top Premier League club at seventeen? He was amazing. At the other end of the spectrum, David Ginola signed at thirty-three. It was near the end for him, but he still had his moments on the field. Some of the things he did in training with his touch and ball control, even someone like me, who has been around, would stand there thinking, 'Oh, my God, you must have been so good. So good.'

If Stan Collymore played in this day and age when there is so much more knowledge and acceptance of depression, and a willingness to talk about it, he would be one of the best players in the world. It's his tragedy career-wise that when you shared your problems back then, there was a lot of unease and scepticism among managers and the press. He had everything: 6 ft 2 in, big, strong, quick, two good feet, excellent in the air and scored goals. The news that he was struggling with depression wasn't received with any real empathy. It was: 'How could you be like that when you earn all that money?' It's nothing to do with money. And sometimes it can be worse if you have money because there is so little sympathy. People think, 'If I had what you have I wouldn't be like that' but you would if you had the same brain. It's an illness. It doesn't matter if you're the richest man in the world or the poorest. Illnesses don't go: 'Oh, wait a minute, he's rich, I'll leave him alone. I'll go for someone poor.' Status doesn't come into it. Mental illness takes nothing like that into consideration.

It's no coincidence that I played my best football at Villa. I had one drink in the entire four years, right at the end of my first marriage in April 1999. The rest of the time I was as sober as a judge. My friend Lee Hendrie, who played with me at Villa, now works with us on *Soccer Saturday* and Sky's midweek shows. I've known Lee for twenty-three years, played with him for four and, in a neat touch, when I played my last match for England in November 1998 and scored in a 2–0 victory over the Czech Republic, it was Lee who made his debut coming on for me as a substitute. He was also one of the main lads in the second series of *Harry's Heroes* and by then I was nearly a year into recovery. Lee said to me the other week, 'You know what, Merse? I've never seen you drunk. I've never seen you have a drink.' It got me thinking. I look back and think of the past as drowning in alcohol because once I started drinking again in 2004, I carried on for almost fifteen years. It's nice to be reminded it wasn't always like that, nice to know that, bar four single nights when I relapsed with booze, 1995 to 2004 were good years for me on the pitch, sober years for me in my life.

If only I could have said the same about gambling.

11

£7 MILLION

Evening games were always a nightmare for me. I could never sleep before a night match and by the turn of the century, there was so much money in the Premier League that when we booked into a hotel at midday on away trips for lunch and a pre-match nap, I would have my own room. After eating we would head up to bed at 1.30 p.m. and get a wake-up call at 4.30 p.m. for tea and toast and the manager's main team-talk before boarding the bus to go to the ground. Those three hours used to wind me up. I'd have all the nervous anticipation of matchday but would be stuck for three hours indoors alone. I would want to get out of my head and blow away the butterflies and doubts. In 2002, Aston Villa were playing Charlton Athletic away and I was on the phone to the bookies for the whole afternoon. It was one bet after another. I was doing it – a grand on this, two grand on that – to win the lost thousand pounds back, but for once I was filled with fear and disgust not *after* the binge when I'd crashed but *during* it. It was like I was a train with no brakes flying down the tracks. I just couldn't stop.

I remember sitting at the foot of my bed in that hotel room and thinking that if I couldn't control the psychological urge to place another bet, I was going to have to take drastic physical action. I felt torn to pieces by the compulsion pulling me one way and the knowledge of all the harm it was doing trying to drag me back in the other direction. Some days, reason is not strong enough to constrain addiction. Later, these would be the kind of moments when killing myself would seem like the only way out, the only refuge from a world of pain. There would come a time when I'd lost heavily and, because I was drinking again by then, the despair overwhelmed me to such an extent that washing down sleeping pills with the vodka seemed the best solution for everyone. Fortunately, I was spared. I woke up and was soon relieved to be alive. But that's where addiction takes you. It's the ultimate victory for something hellbent on destroying you – pushing you to the brink and then over the edge.

Back in the hotel, I came up with another way to stop. What if I broke all my fingers? If I did that, then I couldn't pick up the phone to dial the bookies. Job done. I had a picture in my head of getting a hammer and doing the fingers on my right hand, one by one. But where would I find a hammer? It isn't the sort of thing you can get on room service. I was staring at my hand all this time. What about slamming the fingers in the door? This heavy, self-shutting hotel door would do the trick if I put my hand in the jamb. I sat there contemplating it, feeling it, craving the physical pain, the agony, to distract me from the mental anguish. I was in a daze. Fortunately, the call to go down and get ready for the game stopped me from maiming myself.

I wasn't gambling all the time at Villa but when I did it would quickly spiral until I'd cleaned out my bank account. It was the final straw for my first marriage and would finish my second one, too. It wasn't about the money. Losing £35,000 in a binge was manageable because I was earning big wages. You lose heavily but next month another big lump of money lands in your bank account. The losses themselves are not ruining your home life, because you can still afford to go on holiday when you want and buy everything you need one way or another. Big wages gloss over everything, soften the blow, so you don't pay attention to the scale of your losses. Losing everything I earned, close to £7 million, creeps up on you gradually. You notice it when you no longer have the income to mask it.

What those binges did do, apart from hammer my self-esteem and hollow me out, was make me secretive, defensive and irritable beyond belief. The fear that you're going to be found out, and prove to them what a bad person you are, fuels the paranoia. When they do find out, you're back into a cycle of trying to explain something that is really hard to understand. I don't blame any partner, parent or child of an addict who has relapsed for saying, 'I can't believe you've done it again.' It makes perfect sense to think that way even when they bite their tongue and don't actually say it.

My wife Kate understands me, but it is hard for her and all partners of addicts. She will sometimes say to me, 'Who's that on the phone? Who texted?' My behaviour in the past has caused that suspicion. I get frustrated some days and think, 'Oh my God, I'm fifty-three, someone can ring me and someone can text. It's allowed. It's not a bookie. I'm not having a bet.' On my good days, I accept that it was me, when ill, who has driven her to this. I've made her like that by doing all our money and telling lies constantly. When I'm well, I understand that. I accept it's my behaviour that is to blame.

The toll addiction takes on those who love and live with us messes with their minds almost as much as it twists ours. They're the forgotten sufferers, the forgotten heroes in all this. They start to think it's their fault. 'Why's he done this to me? He doesn't love me. Why isn't he saving to buy a house? It must be because he doesn't want a house. Why doesn't he want a house? Ah! He doesn't want us to be together. Why's he not come home? Why's he always out drinking? Why does he always want to be at the pub with his mates and not with us? Ah! Because he doesn't love me.' They have that thing going on constantly during and after a relapse. They can forgive you because they love you, but it leaves scars. It's hard to convince your family that a lack of love for them has nothing whatsoever to do with it. It's about you and the addiction and while you're chained to it, tragically, so are they.

You don't just hurt yourself in this. The harm you inflict on the people around you isn't seen. That's the side that is neglected, the partner's side, not just when you're on a binge but also when you've started on recovery. My wife can be reeling from the mental pain I've caused, but all of a sudden I can get help and my wife can't. I get well by going to GA and AA and talking to people. I begin a different way of life. I speak to people who help me every day just by listening, by understanding. Recovering addicts need each other. We feed off each other's experiences and support to get well. Who does she speak to? No one. And it does damage, especially as she's gone through all this thinking, 'Is this partly my fault? Is it because of me, he doesn't love me and that's why he keeps doing this, shooting himself in the foot all the time?'

I can't emphasise this enough. It's nothing to do with Kate and if you have an addict in your life, it's nothing to do with you either. You haven't done anything wrong. I love her dearly, but it still didn't stop me doing our savings. It didn't. When all the money has gone I start feeling remorse, but I have to let go. It's done. I can't change what I've done and I know from the past that if I carry the guilt with me all the time, I beat myself up so badly and I'm left in a dangerous place. It's hard for her to let it go, of course. When you talk to someone who isn't addicted, all they can see is the loss. They can't make sense of the numbers, the size of the loss, because it doesn't make sense. The sums are ridiculous. If I was drinking, doing 100 quid in a pub is a lot of money, it would take me all day to get through it. But when gambling and on footballer's wages, I could drop £50,000 in a phone call. Now, logically she knows I'm a compulsive gambler but emotionally she thinks, 'Why would you do that?' She knows I am a good person with an illness but what I've done when ill still really hurts her because it feels like a betrayal of trust.

For me, gambling has always been the cruellest of these addictions, the most difficult to live happily with. That might sound like a weird phrase but this is where the language of addiction is all wrong: 'weak' people who need to become 'strong', 'battles' and 'fights' that can be 'beaten', 'conquered' or 'mastered'. For me, there's no cure, only a coping strategy that becomes more effective the more I talk, the more I share. For my family, gambling is so hideous because they can't see it, the signs of a relapse are not visible until the end. I was going to say 'until it's too late' but it's always too late for the compulsive gambler – a £5 yankee is the start of the road that ends with £10,000 you haven't got riding on your last hope to pull you out of a hole.

I haven't touched cocaine for twenty-seven years but now that people know that I once took it, which only odd strangers did when I was on it, if I relapsed it would be obvious. Never mind the camera phones catching me out, the signs would be there in my eyes and in my manner. If I want to go out and get drunk after two and a half years of being sober, I couldn't hide it. If I walked through the town centre this afternoon after fifteen pints, everyone would know I'd had a drink. If I tried to do it in secret, drinking fifteen pints indoors, upstairs hidden away, running to the toilet all the time, my wife would know by the end of the night.

But if I dropped all my wages in the afternoon and walked through town, no one would have a clue. And if I was at home, sitting on the sofa with my phone out, to all intents and purposes just watching sport on the TV, which is on all the time, every single minute of the day, furtively texting to put bets on, losing God knows how much, no one knows. And that's where the suicidal impulse can sometimes come from, when you've isolated yourself and no one has seen what you've done, the thought of inevitable exposure is so awful, it starts to seem like the only escape route. No one sees it. No one sees that the walls have closed in, the truth has to be faced and you've got nowhere to run until there's no way out.

At Villa, in that hotel room on the road to Charlton, there was always somewhere to run because every month without fail for four years, I'd get a wage slip with a six-figure number on it. I was living on my own for a lot of the time so I would hit the bottom, recognise that only meetings would make me well again and start to get better.

•

These crises raged around my head every few months, but on the field I was calm. Gambling was always the sleeping giant of addictions for me and crossing that white line was the only reliable thing that could knock it out, if only for a couple of hours. Had you only seen me play at Villa and not known my story, you would have thought I was utterly care-free because my genuine enjoyment in the way I was playing was plain to see. It wasn't an act. I just had this ability to lose myself in the game. Off the field I could be on my knees; on it I was always an optimist, ready to seize any opportunity.

We got to the FA Cup final in 2000, the last of them at the old Wembley, but didn't do ourselves justice. I was more out than in the Villa side until December when Lee Hendrie was injured and I got my chance to start an FA Cup tie against Darlington. It was one of those games where everything clicked. I'd been worried beforehand because I was coming up to thirty-two and at that stage of your career you can't just flick it on and off. I needed games to be at my best. Fortunately, though, I played well and I was back in the side for the rest of the season in a new role behind the front two, finishing up as the club's player of the year after only 24 starts. I set up the winner in the fifth-round victory over Leeds United, not that I saw it as Michael Duberry ran into me after I'd headed it back across goal to Benito Carbone and split my forehead open. It was a good move, a dink over Gary Kelly, a knock-up to win the header and I hooked it to Beni to score, worth the six stitches and mild concussion. At Everton in the quarter-final, it was my shot at the end of a slaloming run that was parried to Beni to turn in the winner.

All FA Cup semi-finals now are held at Wembley, of course, but it was an oddity when I played. Mind you, all three of mine were there, understandably so, I suppose, for Arsenal v Spurs, but it felt a bit strange for Villa against Bolton who were in the league below. I shouldn't have played, my back had flared up again but I wasn't going to miss it and we scraped a dour game on penalties. It wasn't much fun to play in, so it must have been poor to watch. I was on the fifth pen but David James' saves meant I wasn't needed.

It was Villa's first FA Cup final since 1957, but we didn't do the occasion justice. We set out to contain them in a midfield battle and my job was to provide crosses for Dion Dublin. I had a volley that whistled over the bar from 25 yards but that was all there was to shout about. When you set out to play like that, there comes a point when you have to kick on and nick it. But it was Chelsea who did that, Gus Poyet pounced on a David James error to win it 1–0. Most of us made more mistakes than David in the match but, as ever with a keeper, one slip can be crucial and his was. I probably took the defeat better than the others. Winning it before does give you a bit of a cushion. It wasn't a day to remember for anyone other than Chelsea's fans and players. As the press wrote, it was a total turkey of a game, as so many FA Cup finals are.

I had asked John Gregory towards the end of that season about extending my contract, which had two years to run, for one more year. I wanted to play to thirty-five and there was nowhere I would rather be than Villa. I wanted to finish my career there and would take a pay cut for the extra, final year but the security would help me weather the expensive divorce I was about to go through. He was reluctant to commit and there were hints in the papers that in fact he wouldn't mind moving me on. At the banquet after the cup final, I mentioned it to Doug Ellis who said, 'You're like a son to me. Don't go. I'll see what I can do.' There isn't much a chairman can do if the manager doesn't fancy keeping you, other than get rid of the manager and John was too good to do that to him. But I turned down an offer to go to Wimbledon in the summer of 2000, resolved to impress the manager and had such a good season that I got the one-year extension and John made me captain when Gareth Southgate was sold to Middlesbrough.

Doug said exactly the same thing to me in the summer of 2002 when Graham Taylor had succeeded John, who had resigned in the January of that year to go to Derby, feeling that the pressure of managing Villa for five years had burned him out. I don't think there was a hangover between me and Graham following my behaviour on the trip to America with England, the so-called Club 18–30 tour. That was ten years in the past. I don't even think it was what I said in that team meeting, when he began talking about what Watford were like in 1977. He just didn't want older players around. David Ginola, Peter Schmeichel and Steve Stone were out of the door pretty sharply, too. Graham favoured younger, impressionable lads. Doug had said to me not to do anything hasty when Graham kept me on the bench throughout pre-season, saying he would have to play me eventually, I was too good to leave out.

I played the second half of an Intertoto Cup victory over FC Zurich at the end of July in front of 18,000 at Villa Park. It wasn't the send-off I'd planned, but a couple of days after the game Graham, who had told me by his actions how I stood, now said it out loud. 'You're not in the team. What are you going to do?' he asked. I replied that I would stay and fight for my place, as Doug had said I was bound to be playing sooner rather than later. Well, that made him mad. 'Look, you've got to go. You're not in my plans,' he said. 'How much do we have to pay you to go?' I reiterated that I didn't want to leave, I'd much rather stay but he said I wouldn't get a sniff while he was manager. Given that he'd only just been appointed – on my recommendation as club captain since he was already on the board and seemed like the best solution – he wasn't going to be leaving for a while. So, I said £100,000, thinking it might make him pause. Doug wouldn't be too happy to write off £100,000. But Graham virtually pulled my hand off, went to see Doug and put it on the line, him or me. I had the cheque within 10 minutes. I was absolutely gutted. I loved that football club – its history, the people, the stadium and supporters. It had a similar vibe to Arsenal with its traditions and class. Villa was the only club that I left in tears. But if the manager doesn't want you, there's not much you can do at thirty-four if playing is your main motivation. I'd had eighteen years of training, the thought of one more year of just that with no meaningful games wasn't for me. I took the money. It didn't go all at once this time, but once I started gambling again I dropped it before I could catch my breath.

•

Harry Redknapp was the first to ring. He had been director
of football at Portsmouth and had taken over as manager
in the summer. Everyone in football knew Pompey were a
basket case, better known as 'Struggling Portsmouth'. They'd
finished in the bottom eight of the Championship for eight
of the last nine seasons and in three of the last four had
needed to win their final game to stay up. Throughout my
career I liked a challenge. I went to Middlesbrough, who had
been relegated, with the mission to get them back up. But
Portsmouth? Bloody hell. It looked like mission impossible.

I was married for the second time, had twin baby girls
and was settled in Birmingham. 'I want you to come down
and be the captain,' said Harry. 'What are they like?' I asked.
'Oh, we're fucking shit,' he said. 'But I've got rid of virtually
everyone, I've got ten players coming in, I want you to be
one of them and we'll give it a right fucking go.' I would
have to take a massive pay-cut, more than fifty per cent, but
I was interested, mainly because of Harry and his attitude.
When I explained that what with the wages and the babies,
I couldn't move to the south coast for that two-year deal and
my body wouldn't handle the drive, he said, 'That's fine, train
two days a week with us and make sure you do the business
on Saturdays and that'll do for me.'

I signed on the Thursday and played the first game of
the season on Saturday, at home against Nottingham Forest,
and we won 2–0. I'd played at Fratton Park once before with
Middlesbrough and knew it as a tight, old-fashioned ground
where the fans are on top of you, it's really hostile and they

make a racket. But that was nothing compared to playing with them on your side. We were limited to 19,000 every week but you would have thought it was five times that size. They never stopped singing and shouting, the bell was ringing all the time and you could feel the noise lifting you. I played in front of far bigger attendances every week for fifteen years and the fans of all the clubs I played for liked to be loud but the dimensions of Fratton Park, and because it felt like it was falling down, added to the fervour. I hadn't played in front of a crowd like that in my life. I had a really good game, got clapped off and thought, 'Here we go.'

Harry is always seen as this wheeler-dealer, as if that's the secret of what he does, buying and selling players. It's nonsense. He's up there with George Graham as a tactician and there's no one better at man-management – if you're in the team. If you're not in the team, he isn't fussed about you at all. He stuck to his word. He never once rowed back from saying, 'It's pointless you training every day, you'll be too tired to kick a ball on Saturday.' I trained Tuesdays and Thursdays, Friday mornings if we were at home, but no other day. If we lost on a Saturday, he wasn't one of those managers who would say, 'Right, you're in on Monday.' His approach was, 'Okay, have your rest and get ready for next week.' I missed one game in forty-six.

Of the ten signings he made, most of us were free transfers: Arjan de Zeeuw, Shaka Hislop, Carl Robinson, Gianluca Festa and later Steve Stone and Tim Sherwood. He also bought Matthew Taylor, Deon Burton and Richard

Hughes for small fees and then the Nigeria striker Yakubu for £4 million in the run-in. This was no supermarket sweep. He bought everyone in their positions. He didn't just get ten players in and scratch his head and go, 'Where am I going to play them?' People who give him a hard time as a 'wheeler-dealer', remember you only do that sort of business at Portsmouth if you know what you're doing, if you know football.

Because I'd signed just before the first game, I hadn't trained. That was a stark reminder that I wasn't at Villa or Boro and especially Arsenal anymore. The facilities were more like Brentford and the pitch itself wasn't full size. After my first session, I did what I always did and threw my dirty training kit into the middle of the floor. You're allocated a number, it's on all your bits and bobs, you pile them all up and the next morning it's all clean and rolled up in your place, ready for you to train again. But once I'd lobbed mine on to the floor, the lads started laughing. 'What are you doing?' one of them said. 'We wash our own kit here.'

I couldn't believe it. 'You're having a laugh? Clean your own kit? This is the Championship, not non-league.' I thought, 'I've come here from Villa, come here to achieve something. If we go up I'm on a £250,000 bonus, which makes it worthwhile me taking such a big pay-cut. But how can I do that if we're treated like a pub team?' I said, 'What happens then because I'm not cleaning my own kit?' Turns out that everyone cleaned their own kit because the other option was paying Big Kevin, the kitman, thirty quid a week to do it for them. So, because I had the hump I said to Big Kevin, who's still there now, 'Clean my kit for nothing. And if we go up, I'll give you ten grand.' He was well up for that. Of course, we went up and I had to give him ten grand – I only trained twice a week and it ended up costing me ten grand. Biggest laundry bill ever.

After Forest we drew with Sheffield United then went to Crystal Palace. We were losing 2–0 at half-time. Dougie Freedman had ripped us to shreds. I remember walking off at the break thinking, 'What the fuck have I done? Is this what it's going to be like? Are we one of those teams who'll win at home with that crowd behind us but we'll get battered every game away? I hope it's not like that, or worse, typical Portsmouth, a relegation battle. At my age. That's not for me.' I sat in the dressing room, all gloomy and angry. But Harry just pointed at Gary O'Neil and Carl Robinson and said, 'You off and you off, you two are coming on, we're going three at the back, Merse, you go in the hole and let's go.' We scored three times in four second-half minutes, one of the subs, Jason Crowe, getting two of them. That was the moment. We were a team that wasn't used to winning. That's why I feared for us at half-time. It's hard when the players haven't experienced winning matches regularly. They lacked the knowhow but Harry's tactical switches solved all that.

We went on a roll. With all the players, we were miles too good for that league. It was ridiculous. We were beating teams by three or four goals. It was just a pleasure to play in that side. But I could only play in it because Harry looked after me. We used Vincent Pericard, Yakubu and Svetoslav Todorov up front, forwards who were Premier League quality. With Todorov, I didn't even have to look. I'd just get the ball and put it into the most dangerous place and he'd always be there. I scored 12 and he scored 26. It's nice that Linvoy Primus said that I was a transformational signing, the one that showed them how to become a good team but, like anyone, I was only as good as the players around me. I was fortunate to be surrounded with really good players and everybody played out of their skin. There was not a single player who didn't raise their game – Tim Sherwood, Premier League winner, Shaka Hislop in goal and Steve Stone, who played in the Euros for England, the Forest side that finished third and with me at Villa. We weren't all veterans: Matty Taylor and Gary O'Neil were kids who were flying all season, and as for Linvoy, my nan probably had more chance of playing than Linvoy when I got there. Yet he was our best player that season and deservedly ended up player of the year.

It was the most enjoyable season of my career. I wasn't drinking and, at the beginning, I was well. The gambling addiction though kicked in big time as the season went on, like it did at Middlesbrough in another promotion season. Come the spring and the tension cranks up and gambling always was the distraction I craved most. I remember us playing Wimbledon at Selhurst Park in the March. We were top, smashing everybody. They were 17th. I think we were 5–6 to win the game and I rang up and put £50,000 on us. I scored from about 20 yards to put us 1–0 up and I thought, 'This is handy'. But we got beaten 2–1. We only lost three away games all season and that was one of them, the one I put a bet on. I'll never forget it. I didn't have the money to lose. So it taught me not to have another bet . . . until the next time.

Harry tells a story from the match before the Wimbledon defeat and most of it is true. I had thirty grand on me before the game to settle a gambling debt after the match. I asked him while we were getting changed when the valuables bag, where you put your watches, wallets and chains, would be going into the Millwall safe. 'It ain't', he said. 'They've had a robbery. We'll just put it in the kit skip and shut the lid. It'll be all right'. I said, 'You're joking? I've got something I can't leave in there'. He said he would look after it and then nearly fainted when I gave him thirty grand in readies. He stuffed the bundles down his tracksuit trousers and wrote in his autobiography that they moved about so much when he stood up to give us instructions that he doubled up so one wouldn't fall down his leg, spill on to the touchline and cause a riot as everyone piled in to get a £50 note. All our bench thought he had stomach ache and tried to persuade him to leave the dug-out and go to see the doc.

I played 795 games in club and international football. That was the best I ever played. We won 5–0. Everything I did came off. I'd pass the ball and I would stand there and think, 'How's that got there?' There was no thinking, just doing and it all clicked. I've never been in a game like it. At the end, with about five minutes to go, Harry brought me off and I got a standing ovation. That's rare but not totally inconceivable. This was Millwall fans who were on their feet because our supporters had been banned apart from a handful in corporate hospitality. Walking out of the Den after the game, there was an old bloke in his seventies waiting and he asked me to sign something for him. He said, in a thick Bermondsey accent, 'I've been coming darn 'ere since I was seven years of age, son, and I've never seen a performance like that in my life. No away player has ever got a standing ovation here, son.' That has always stuck with me, a great end to a perfect day.

The other anecdote Harry tells about me shows how clever and subtle he could be. After we had lost to Manchester United in the FA Cup third round, I knew we would have a free weekend when the next round was played. I wanted some time off so I told him I was struggling with my gambling and wanted to go into Tony Adams' Sporting Chance clinic in Hampshire for a week for treatment. He was great and gave me the time off. It was true that I was betting heavily again, but I had a different solution. Rather than going into rehab, all I needed was to get away and I reckoned a week on the beach with the family would stop me from blowing thousands at the bookies. I took my wife and twins to Barbados for the week, coming back with the deepest January tan you could imagine. While I was out there a bloke walked over to me one day at the shops and said, 'Hello, Merse. How are you? It's going great at Pompey isn't it? Harry's got you lot going . . .' I stopped and had a chat, thinking nothing more of it.

When I got back, Harry turned a blind eye to the tan. Never mentioned it. Nor that the bloke I'd been chatting to was a friend of one of his best mates, the billionaire race-horse owner, Michael Tabor. Apparently, he had rung him up that night and said he'd just had a chat with 'one of your Portsmouth lads, Paul Merson'. Harry got the wrong end of the stick and started to console him about going into treatment, asking what had forced him into Sporting Chance. 'Drink? Please say, not the drugs?' The bloke asked him what he was on about and said he'd met me in Barbados.

'The cheeky sod,' said Harry.

I didn't know he knew for years. I went on *Goals on Sunday* about six years later with him and he told the story, though he nearly dropped me right in it when he said I'd told him I needed treatment because I had a problem with 'gambling and birds'. I never said I had a problem with women, it wasn't true and I wouldn't have said it. Maybe that was his payback to try to drop me in it with my ex-wife . . . Harry and I could have had a big row, he could have easily fined me two weeks' wages, which is what John Gregory did to me four years earlier. But he took a different view. 'What's the point?' he thought. 'If I do that, I'm going to lose him. He'll get the hump about the money and being found out and be on a massive sulk-up on Saturday. As long as he turns it on for me on Saturday, I don't care. I just don't care.' That's incredible man-management. He read me perfectly. And to keep the story under his hat for such a long time shows you what a shrewd bloke he is.

We strolled to promotion, 18 points clear of third place and the day it was confirmed, when we beat Burnley on 15 April, was the most memorable moment of my career, the one I can still see in my mind, clear as a bell. I missed a penalty that night at 0–0, but the crowd was electric and never stopped roaring us on. 'Play up, Pompey!' could be heard on the Isle of Wight. When Todorov scored the winner it felt like the roof was coming off. With everything I'd won before, I was always preoccupied about what we were going to do next, worried about the celebration rather than savouring the achievement, 'Right, let's get pissed.' When all the fans ran on at the end, I was lifted onto the shoulders of one of the security guards and just sucked it all in. And I thought, 'This will never happen to me again. This time, take it all in. It doesn't get better than this.' I can talk to Perry Groves about 1989 and he can reel off 1,500 stories about that night once we'd left Anfield and honestly I don't remember any of them. But the day we beat Burnley to seal promotion, it's like yesterday. I was so lucky, I was fit every week because I had a manager who accepted that a thirty-five-year-old knew what was best for his body.

It is the most fulfilled I've ever felt on a football field. To think how rotten Portsmouth had been for years, we were rank outsiders to win the league. We were like the Leicester City of 2016, but of the Championship. There was such a sense of satisfaction that I'd been challenged to achieve something when written off by Graham Taylor and I'd managed to do it. It also proved a point to him as Villa slumped from eighth to sixteenth, forcing his resignation. The only disappointment in the entire year was my decision not to turn up to the end of season parade, which I deeply regret. My son had a big football tournament on the Sunday and I chose to go to that instead. How often do you get parades? Kids' football tournaments come left, right and centre. I look back now and wish I had gone. Back then I had a ruthlessly professional outlook when it came to the club. I thought, 'You've given me a job to get promoted and I've done that. I haven't let a soul down.' I put my family first, but I was wrong to do that. It was a huge shame, especially given I was captain, although I never intended it to be a snub to anyone. I should have been there and I'm so sorry that I wasn't.

12

ROCK BOTTOM

The BBC has footage of me somewhere as a Premier League player with Portsmouth. Not from a match, because I never played in the top flight again, but film of me as captain for the opening credits of *Match of the Day* juggling the ball in Pompey's baggy royal blue shirt. It was never used. I had a year left on my contract, but the more I thought about it, the more convinced I was that I'd literally be out of my league.

I was thirty-five, plus the gulf between promoted sides and the established clubs is unreal. Some teams might come up and do all right for a season, but more times than not they'll struggle. It hit me how hard it would be in the Premier League for someone of my age coming towards the end. I was always an honest player and understood that the Championship was now my level. I was trapped – I wouldn't be fit enough to play in the Premier League training twice a week but my body and mind couldn't take full-time training because my wife and the twins were settled in Birmingham. I had to leave. I owed it to everyone, not least myself, to go and Harry was brilliant about it, agreeing to release me if I could get a club back in the West Midlands. Because he brought in thirty-seven-year-old Teddy Sheringham to replace me, Portsmouth fans sometimes ask whether I'd done myself down, that at two years younger than Ted I could have coped. I really don't think so: I would have needed a different body and different mind.

West Bromwich Albion wanted me. They had just been relegated and the chief executive called and asked me to join. There couldn't have been a better option – I loved the Hawthorns as a ground, they were a proper, traditional club, on my doorstep, had good players and were one of those clubs that hadn't wasted all their money in the Premier League so were always going to be around the top of the Championship. It was a surprise, because they would have been ideal but for one thing. 'Brilliant,' I said. 'I'd definitely be up for signing. Is Gary Megson okay with it?' It wasn't a shock to hear the CEO say, 'Hmm. Gary's still on holiday and we haven't spoken to him about it yet, but *we* want you.'

I said, 'I can't sign. I need the manager to want me first.' I agreed to hold off talking to other clubs until they had contacted Megson, but I knew it wasn't going to happen. I wasn't his kind of player. I hadn't got the legs anymore to chase the ball into corners and play at 100 mph. By that stage, I needed the ball to feet in midfield, not fighting for scraps off knockdowns. As I said to the CEO, 'He won't want me. I'm a bit of a luxury player these days.' All I could say when he rang me back to inform me that Gary didn't fancy me at West Brom was, 'I told you.'

Then Walsall came in for me. They were about to start their third year in the Championship and had finished 18th and 17th in the previous two. I met the chairman, Jeff Bonser, and the manager, Colin Lee, and told them about my year at Portsmouth. 'I trained Tuesdays and Thursdays and played all those games. I played some of my best football and because I'm getting on, that's what I need.' And they said, 'Not a problem, we'll do that.' So I signed. It was top whack for Walsall, another hefty pay-cut for me but it wasn't about the money, it was about being looked after. I saw what they'd done the year before. They had lost 22 games and I said to them, 'If we can turn seven of those defeats into wins, it would have been good enough to get into the play-offs last season. You never know.'

Our first game of the season, coincidentally, was West Brom at home. It was a scorching day, 38 degrees C, and I scored two very good first-half goals, a volley from 18 yards into the top left corner and a shot from the edge of the D that crashed in off the underside of the crossbar. We won 4–1, but it wasn't a hammering. West Brom were at it all day, making dozens of chances. Everybody was buzzing afterwards, someone called me 'the Messiah' on the telly but I had to say it as I saw it. There was too much hype and far too soon. 'If we finish above West Brom this year, we will be promoted,' I said. I was right. West Brom won the league, we got relegated.

We had some decent players: Vinny Samways, who had won the cup with Tottenham, was the same age as me and hardly ever gave the ball away but he was commuting . . . from Spain; Steve Corica and Simon Osborn were coming towards the end of really good careers after long spells at Wolves; Paul Ritchie had played at a high level; you wouldn't want to be marked by Jamie Lawrence; Jimmy Walker was a top goalie; Matty Fryatt was a young, smart centre-forward, and Jorge Leitao was 'the one-man Portuguese army' up front. We drew the next two and I scored the equaliser at Stoke, but then the bubble burst.

Straight after that we lost four and drew one of our next five games. Midway through that dismal run, Colin asked to have a word. Some of the players had gone in to see him and said, 'How come we're in on a Sunday after we get beaten and Merse isn't in?' There are two ways of dealing with that. He could have said, 'I'm the manager. He's thirty-five and the captain, he's won everything in the game and this is how to get the best out of him.' Instead he went the other way. 'It's not really working,' he said to me. 'The players are starting to get the hump now because you're only in a couple of days a week. I can't have that. I need you to come in.' It's that 'one size fits all' mentality again.

Bryan Robson and Harry Redknapp could easily have gone the same way as Colin Lee. They didn't because they were phenomenal man-managers. They didn't need to see me out there every day doing the work just to show the others that everyone was treated the same. I'm not saying I was entitled to do less, only that running me into the ground Monday to Friday was no way to get someone pushing thirty-six at his sharpest. Colin was a coach, and a very good one too. He wasn't a top manager. It's a different kind of thing. When the team is read out on Friday and you're not playing, the coach puts his arm round you. The coach is someone who comes to you and says, 'Don't worry. You'll be in the team soon.' The coach is everyone's friend. The manager has got to pick eleven and keep the other eleven happy, and that's not as easy as people think. Colin didn't have that authority with the players, didn't feel comfortable putting his foot down and telling them, 'No, he won the league last year doing that. I trust him to perform.' He melted and had me in every day. By the time the game came on Saturday, I was exhausted. I was atrocious.

Everywhere I played, I know I'm lucky to get a good reception when I go back. At Arsenal, Aston Villa, Portsmouth, even Middlesbrough, despite leaving under a cloud, when they talk about players they'll put me up there as one of the better ones they've seen. It's lovely to be thanked and praised like that. Sit down with a load of Walsall fans and they would probably say, 'He's useless.' I'm sure I wouldn't get into their top 20 footballers who have played for the club. That early, great form I arrived with from Portsmouth fizzled out because by the time a full week's training had ended, I was knackered. I was picked but I hardly scored. My legs were shot from all the running and I was shit. There was a massive difference in the quality of players, too. In the position I played later in my career, out wide or in the hole, I was only ever as good as the players up front. I relied on them – if you're threading the ball through and they're putting it wide you're not getting the accolades for having the vision to find the pass. At Walsall, the players obviously weren't as good as the likes of Alan Smith, Ian Wright, John Hartson, Marco Branca, Dion Dublin, Svetoslav Todorov. And if they weren't as good, they weren't going to make me look good. When you're flicking balls around the corner, if no one has tuned in and doesn't make the right run, it's you who looks the idiot.

It was the decision to make me train every day that destroyed me. I would get the hump and, because I couldn't keep a lid on the frustration, the injustice of the manager going back on his word, I would sometimes just catch the ball while we were doing finishing or during an eight-a-side, boot it down the road and storm off the pitch. Colin used to call me into his office and try to get me to calm down. He once said, 'I've just been on the phone to Kevin Keegan because I don't know how to deal with you, I've never worked with someone like you before.' Kevin had said to him, 'As long as they're doing the business on Saturdays, those sort of players, you let them get on with it.' It was pure common sense. But Colin had backed the others over me and wouldn't climb down.

When I got there, I was still buzzing about Saturdays. All the training and banter through the week is great if you're playing well and in a good dressing room, but as the end of your career approaches, Saturday is all that counts. No point being sensational on a Tuesday morning. But now the enjoyment of Saturday had gone. At Walsall, that hour and a half, which had always been my release, my space to enjoy my life, to be me, was almost unbearable. I couldn't do what I used to be able to do and emotionally I started to fall apart. I would come off the pitch feeling I was rubbish. Even at my worst with the addictions, I knew I could play. Now the thing that had propped up my self-worth for so long was fading away, because I was tired before kick-off and the passes I did play weren't being read. I couldn't get out of trouble anymore.

I could not cope with sitting there with my feelings, dwelling on how badly I'd played. In my early days, with the high that I got from playing well, I always wanted to keep that going when I came off the pitch. But I couldn't just go home because I couldn't stop my mind racing, couldn't decelerate from a million miles an hour to the pace of normal living. I stayed at top speed until I ran out of road and crashed. After the final whistle up to 1994, I'd walk up the tunnel thinking, 'Shit, what now?' And the answer was to chase the buzz with gambling, drink and drugs. Now it was the other way round. I wasn't maintaining the high. There *was* no high. I hated myself for playing so poorly and I needed to chase the blues away. I was desperate for a pick up. When you're low, the compulsion is in your ear all the time. 'Have a bet,' it says. 'You know you love having a bet. It'll make you feel better. You'll win some money, that'll cheer you up. Why make yourself miserable? Go on, have a bet. You deserve this.' I thought, 'I know, I'll have a bet.'

That's how I started on the most ruinous binge of my life. It had taken four months from winning the league with Portsmouth for my career to fall to earth. Within another twelve months I would be cleaned out, my second marriage was all over bar the shouting, I had been into rehab, relapsed spectacularly and was wrecking my dream of being a manager. Everything went. I'd put sixty grand on a match, lose it and then put eighty grand on another to try to claw the sixty grand back. I'd have fifteen grand on Federer to win a single match and then put ten grand on the first batsman to be out in a day's play at the Test. It was insane. The promotion bonus was gone in days. I'm coming towards the end of my career, the wages are going down but the stakes I'm punting are going up, because only serious risk will do the trick now for me. I was dicing with danger everywhere. I could no longer get out of trouble on the pitch and in gambling terms, I was running out of ammunition. When you're on big money you always have a chance. Rock bottom for the compulsive gambler on Premier League wages is like a trampoline, you can usually bounce back because another 100 grand is coming next month. When you're on Walsall wages, that's when it all goes tits up.

And then the worst thing that could have happened to me came through my letterbox. It was a letter from the PFA saying that since I had now turned thirty-five, I was eligible to access my pension which, I was informed, could be done in a number of ways. One of them was to take it as a lump sum. It totalled about £750,000. I didn't even know I had it, let alone was able to draw the whole lot out. You know that character on *The Fast Show*, the 13th Duke of Wybourne? His catchphrase is, 'With my reputation? What were they thinking?' I can't help but feel like that now. Who was looking out for me? Who was helping me? How could they let that happen? The very last thing I should be receiving is a letter saying you've got all this money and, by the way, do you want it all now? The PFA knew my story. They'd been part of the process of sending me to rehab nine years before. I wasn't Joe Bloggs, I was the most well-known and serious addict in the game. How could they do that to someone with, famously, so much form? It was supposed to last me the rest of my life but there was no, 'Hold on a minute, this boy's career is coming to an end. If he manages another year or two to thirty-seven he's going to do well, then he's got the next fifty years. Let's think what we're going to do here. We're going to offer an addict the £750,000 he has saved and built up over nineteen years, the only part of his income that has always been protected from his compulsion, now? What's he going to do with that? If he throws it away, there's no more. How would he live his life in the future without everything he's saved to fall back on?' Surely someone puts two and two together and says, 'Wait there . . .'

There was no dialogue, no advice, no thought of duty of care. Nothing.

Someone like me, whose brain when it comes to betting is not wired right, is always taking the lot. You're only going to do one thing. Which compulsive gambler isn't?

I know that people will say, 'You were old enough. Your fault, tough shit.' I get that. But when you're a compulsive gambler you don't think days ahead, never mind fifty years into the future. All you're thinking about is the next bet. I think it was negligent. Now an agent, accountant or solicitor might step in. The union is more aware as well, and if that's because of me, who was left to my own devices to spunk the lot, as an example of how you have to take steps to safeguard the addicted from their compulsive behaviour, that is some comfort.

Those months when I lost everything are a haze. Like an alcoholic's blackout, in the real depths of a gambling binge, I was on another planet. Only fragments remain. Earlier that year, I had been unaware for weeks that the Iraq war had started because I was in my own world. I could function as a footballer, go into training, but I was like a zombie in the rest of my life, glued to the telly and Teletext at all hours of the day and night. Some moments it would hit me hard and I would think only of killing myself, the rest of the time I would banish those thoughts with another bet, always trying to salvage the mess I'd made.

By February I was out of my mind, a serious danger not just to my savings but to my own life. I didn't want my kids to live with the knowledge that I'd taken my own life. But this was no life I was leading, no life worth living. We had cancelled Sky at home and I'd surrendered my mobile phone in an attempt to put up a barrier between me and the bookies, but I just used phone boxes instead. At the very end of my tether, with my wife unable to stop me falling over the edge because I was incapable of listening when the compulsion drowned out every sane voice, I spoke to our chairman, Jeff Bonser. And like Ken Friar at Arsenal, this kind and practical man worked selflessly to pull me back from the brink. He rang the PFA and between them they got me a place at residential rehab, Sierra Tucson in Arizona. It was £20,000 a month. I could no longer afford it. I've never seen anyone go into treatment or come to GA meetings and say, 'My name's so-and-so and I'm a compulsive gambler. I've come in because I'm sick of winning.' When you go in, it's because you've done your bollocks. The time when you most need intensive, life-saving private therapy, because public provision is so badly underfunded, is the moment you're least equipped to pay for it. Walsall sorted it and I paid them back with deductions from my wages over the length of my contract.

I was as reluctant as the last time. I didn't want to fly, I didn't want to abandon my family, I couldn't afford it and I was worried about leaving Walsall, who were tumbling down the table, in the lurch. The PFA sent Jim Walker, my former physio at Aston Villa and confidant of Paul McGrath when he was at the club and suffering terribly with his alcoholism, as a chaperone to make sure I didn't do a bunk. It was a very calm and peaceful place, in the middle of nowhere and I undertook four weeks of intensive therapy and treatment. There were quite a few recognisable faces in there with me, but you put fame to one side and concentrate on the illness.

I hadn't taken drugs for coming up to ten years, hadn't had a drink for five. I spoke about what had happened, my life-long struggles with gambling and, unlike the first time, we focused intently on that one addiction.

Sierra Tucson was unreal compared with Marchwood. The understanding of gambling, 'the secret addiction' as they called it, was streets ahead of where it had been ten years before. One day towards the end of my month's stay, I sat down with one of the counsellors, him at one side of a small table, me at the other. He said that in this session he would be my addiction and talk to me as if it were the compulsion itself possessing him and addressing me. It sounds weird but it was so scary. 'I'm waiting for you. I'm waiting. I'll kill you in the end.' It was chilling. I cried my eyes out because I could always feel the addiction inside me and now it was there in front of me, come to life. It's a shame my family weren't with me because they could have seen the pain and torment of what it's like to be haunted by this. They would have seen my demons rather than what they saw as 'weaknesses'. Instead of understandably only seeing what my gambling had done to them, they would have seen what it did to me.

When the month was up, I thought I had a better under-standing of it. I had lasted a whole month without a bet. The feeling of hopelessness had gone, I was healthy, lively, off the floor and I felt lighter. I was ready to fly home. 'It is against our advice,' my psychiatrist said. 'You are the worst patho-logical gambler I've ever encountered. We think you need nine months' treatment.' There was no way I could afford that and, in any case, I was missing the children too much. She said they could sort out an apartment for me, a job to pay the rent and I could go to sessions there in the evening. 'Don't' go,' she said, 'you really aren't well.' I wasn't having it. I needed to work and see my kids. The crisis was over, I thought. I could not have been more wrong. If I'd stayed for another nine months, I don't think I'd have had the next fifteen years of pain.

•

I held it together for a while. I had missed six games while I was in Arizona, three draws and three defeats that had sent us down to 21st place. I came back as a second-half sub on 13 March in a victory over Wimbledon, our first win since Boxing Day. The chairman sacked Colin Lee a month later when, with four games to go, we were 19th and two points above the relegation zone. Jeff Bonser had put me in rehab twelve weeks before, so no one was more surprised than me that he asked me to take the team for the rest of the season. He just said, 'Go and do it for me.' He had seen me at my most fragile and had the evidence in his office, the mobile phones I'd smashed up and jumped on fifty times after a gambling binge. He would have thought, as I had hoped, that Arizona had put a stop to all that. I'd always wanted to be a football manager. I knew it was an incredible opportunity and one I was unlikely to be given anywhere else. You can't really choose your first job, it chooses you, and fate would have it that I was in the right place at the wrong time.

A sense of heavy responsibility in a relegation battle dominates your every thought as a manager. The pressure comes when you recognise that people are depending on you for their livelihoods – not the players, they will have their contracts honoured come what may – the future of dozens of members of staff is in your hands. You go down and there will be cutbacks. People will lose their jobs. There's no 'bounce straight back' for them. And let's be honest, Walsall were punching above their weight in that league. They're a great little club, really well run and never going belly up. They have a core of 5,000 dedicated fans. At three years this was already their longest spell in the second tier but they didn't have the gates or money to live in the Championship indefinitely. The bottom half of League One, top half of League Two, is their natural level but that's not to say we didn't bust a gut in those four games to try to stay up.

I picked the wrong team for my first game against Norwich. That was my fault. They were going up as champions, we were on a bit of a hiding to nothing so I thought we'd attack them with three forwards. We made chances but we lost 5–0. Back to 4–4–2 for Sheffield United away: we lost 1–0 to a penalty. I went even more defensive against Crystal Palace, who would be promoted via the play-offs, and we played well yet still went down 1–0 to an 88th minute goal. That defeat put us in 22nd, the last relegation place with one to play. We needed to beat Rotherham at home and hope that Stoke would defeat Gillingham at the Britannia Stadium, which I thought they would do – they were ten places higher and Tony Pulis, the home side's manager, had left Gillingham after a row with the owner. We won 3–2 in front of what remains the Bescot Stadium's record attendance, 11,049. It was one of those games that can give you a heart attack. We were winning 2–1 with 90 minutes on the clock when the referee gave them their second dubious penalty of the match and then we fought back again in injury-time to score the winner. It didn't make any difference: Gillingham drew at Stoke and we went down on goal difference. We were unlucky. Walsall finished on 51 points; no club for eight years had been relegated with as many.

Jeff, bless him, had seen and heard enough to offer me the job on a full-time basis. I wish I'd done justice to his decision. Management is hard enough when you're well. It occupies all your thoughts all the time. But when you're ill? Really, I had no chance. It didn't take long for my addictions to start snowballing again. When I got back from America, I moved back in with my wife, Louise. She had been teetotal since the day I met her to help me, but when I was away she had started drinking again and, quite reasonably, said, 'You've gambled away everything, so what if I have a drink?' I just thought, 'You know what? I'll join you.' I swapped one addiction for another straightaway. For five years I'd said to myself, 'I'm gambling but at least I'm not drinking.' Now, for a while, it was the opposite. I could never get the balance right. It had been five years since my last relapse and ten since I was a regular boozer, but it was like I'd never stopped. It was an eye-opener for her because she'd never seen me drink and there I was running up the road to the off licence to buy a bottle of wine and coming home to drink it before saying, 'Let's have another bottle.' And I'd be back up the road. I went off on a mad one again. We split up once and for all pretty quickly after that and I was back living on my own.

Only a few weeks earlier, I had confronted my addiction over a table in Arizona. It had scared me to death but I went back to it not long after I had started drinking again. It's like a snake. 'You'll be all right, Paul,' it hisses. 'It'll be different this time.' It's never different but knowing that wouldn't stop me. That summer my 'secret addiction' was all over the *News of the World*. I had an account with Stan James at the time. Their invision service was on pages 663–664 on Channel 4 Teletext. I would come in at night and put a big bet on basketball or baseball and watch the market, not the match. I could tell you who was on base, who was coming in to bat, by the way the prices fluctuated. One Sunday, they printed the details of my account's recent activity: £20,000 on the LA Lakers to beat the Detroit Pistons, £6,000 on Pittsburgh Pirates to win, £12,000 on Anaheim Angels, £10,000 on the Yankees, £3,500 on Michael Owen to be top-scorer at Euro 2004, £10,000 on a Yorkshire cricket match, £9,000 on Castleford Tigers. They listed more than 100 grand's worth of losing bets over a six-week period.

I rang the company up. 'What's happening? I shouldn't be gambling, I've just come out of treatment. I bet with you because of the privacy.' They said they were really sorry, saying they thought it was an inside job, someone stealing confidential information and selling it to the paper. The top man rang me back to apologise, saying he was really sorry. 'What do you mean?' I said. 'What if you get me the sack at Walsall? What are you going to do about it?' He said that I had lost about 100 over the period and that they would refund it to me but close my account. I don't know if I was entitled to a fortune for a data breach but I took it. It was my biggest 'win'. Somehow the last bit of my pension had been saved. What did I do? I opened up a credit account with someone else and lost it all . . . and more.

•

I had one full season as Walsall's player-manager, one chance at a brilliant opportunity and it was spoilt by the gambling, the drinking and a lack of experience. I knew I had pretty good ideas. I wanted to go with the young players, give them a chance like I'd been given a chance. When you do that, you need patience. We had been quite negative under Colin, but that was because he was an accomplished coach who had been around long enough to know we didn't have the talent to open football matches up. He had the experience to tighten it up and think that if the fans didn't like it, they would have to lump it. He would not be swayed, because he was confi-dent he knew what he was talking about. I came in and said, 'We're going to play attacking football.' I didn't want to sit on the bench and watch boring nil-nils, but you have to play to the strengths of your team, you can't play to the crowd because when it goes wrong it's down to you not them, you're supposed to know what you're doing. I lacked the experience as a manager but not on the pitch. I should have played more, it always seemed to help when I was out there.

I appointed young coaches in Simon Osborn and Iffy Onuora, who were both very good at their jobs, top lads. We won one, drew three and lost one of the first five games and the chairman thought we needed an older head. I brought in Frank Barlow who had been a manager in his own right years before and then worked as the assistant to Trevor Francis and Danny Wilson. He was up there with Steve Harrison of Aston Villa and England as a training-ground coach. I may have played 700-odd games and won leagues, cups and promotions, but when Frank was talking and taking a session, I'd hang on his every word. He laid firmer foundations for us and, when he left to go to Nottingham Forest with Gary Megson, I employed Jim Walker, who was a massive help to me. He had always been someone I could confide in at Villa, a football man who listened and never judged.

It was up and down all season. We lost five matches in a row in March and then, having signed Julian Joachim and Andrew Surman on loan, we won our last five games of the season to finish 14th. That was my happiest time in management. We went to Hartlepool, who were flying, and smashed them 3–1. For the briefest spell, I must have felt like Pep Guardiola feels most of the time, sitting and watching in supreme confidence: 'We're winning today. I know we're winning. These are good players, this is a good team, who's going to beat us?'

Throughout that season, my addictions were raging. I wasn't right. I would fill a Lucozade bottle with vodka and orange and drink from it while watching reserve games. I regret it so much. I feel I let myself down. The addictions would have stopped me being a success anywhere. If, by some stroke of impossible luck, I had been appointed manager of Liverpool when my addictions were rife, I wouldn't have lasted 10 minutes.

The addict is a perfectionist and when things aren't perfect that's the excuse to fall back on drinking or gambling or whatever. It's hard relying on other people to prove your worth. It's a great buzz when you win, better I think than when you win as a player because you have had a whole week of planning and work, you've outwitted the other manager and got your players playing the way you wanted. That's when it's dangerous for me. When there was such a buzz, I had to prolong it. I couldn't go home and switch off. I could not bring myself down from that buzz to normality. If we lost, I'd want to obliterate the low. There's a saying, 'I'll have a drink when I'm happy or sad. Whether the sun is shining or it rains.' As an alcoholic I would drink when and because it was sunny, I'd drink when and because it was raining. There was no normal. If we'd won, I'd drink myself silly. If we lost, I'd drink myself silly.

When you're behaving like that, you don't carry the aura you need to be a successful manager. People are looking up to you, but if you think you're worthless, it's difficult to persuade others that you're worthwhile. When you carry yourself well, you project 'I'm a good player and a good manager'. Once you're drinking and gambling as a relapsed addict and your self-worth is on the floor, that's going to affect how you're perceived. It takes everything from you. How can anyone feed off you when you're just a shell of a man?

It has other consequences too. You start to question whether you can tell a player off. You think, 'I can't say anything bad, how can I criticise him when I'm living my life like this?' You let people off when you need to come down hard because you know what you are. You also want everybody to love you, you're desperate for any feelgood feedback, to be Mr Nice when the last thing a manager can be all the time is Mr Nice. When you love yourself, it doesn't matter who doesn't like you. When you hate yourself, if one person doesn't like you, it's difficult to take – you start thinking they're all talking about you behind your back now, and you start to worry.

Those thoughts would never enter your head when you love yourself. Take training, for instance. I hadn't set the greatest example as a player at Walsall because of my frustrations at being made to go in every day. And when I took the manager's job, the players looked at me and thought, 'Well, you didn't train hard.' No one there trained like I did for most of my career. I trained as hard as anyone when I was at Arsenal. The footballers I played with later in my career may think I was an atrocious trainer. It's true, unless we were playing eight v eight, I wouldn't want to know, but that was because I had earned the right to determine what was best for my body as I approached the end of playing. Without the drinking, and had I given up playing and not had to train in a different way to them, I would have had the confidence to tell them to ignore what I was doing and do what I was saying. Instead, I was paranoid that they might think I was a hypocrite.

There's a great camaraderie among managers. You could ring just about anyone up and they would take your call to chat about players and how it was going. When Mick McCarthy would ask if I was enjoying it, at the start I'd say, 'I don't like Mondays to Fridays but I love Saturdays.' He would laugh: 'You wait . . . give it a couple of months and you'll look forward to Monday to Friday and dread Saturdays.' He was spot on.

•

When the 2004–05 season finished, the loan players went back to their clubs and the ones heading out of contract had been offered more money or a longer deal somewhere else. We weren't great payers and the team that had won five on the trot was broken up. I didn't have the money to make the signings that would have transformed the side. I rang up a good centre-forward, told him I wanted to take him, how much I rated him, offered him our highest salary, £1,200 a week, and he said, 'I'd love to play for you, Paul.' But he also said Sheffield Wednesday had offered him £2,500 a week. I said, 'Don't even think about it. You sign for them.' It wasn't just being unable to recruit the quality in depth we needed, we were a club that had to sell its best players, too. Matty Fryatt was a fabulous striker for us, but when Leicester City offered £750,000, it was goodnight and I could not replace like for like.

Jeff Bonser was brilliant to deal with, really understanding and supportive. But he had control and power over me because gambling had removed any possibility I could protest strongly about budgets and sales. He would sell every player in sight to ensure the club survived. I understood that but my debts took away my freedom of action. When he told me he needed to sell a couple of players, I wasn't in a position financially to say, 'I can't stay if you do that.' I needed the job. Gambling did that to me, not him. Managers who can threaten to walk away have got enough to live on. The rest of us knuckle down and hope for the best, fearing the worst – that only the manager carries the can for sales.

There were games before I left the club during that second season when I would get up on a Saturday morning and think, 'We have got no chance today. None.' Everywhere I'd played before, I'd been a hero. Now I was a villain because there were stretches when we couldn't buy a win. For the only time in my life, I was getting stick from the crowd. We played Bristol City away one Monday night. We had injuries and I played a lot of kids. We lost 3–0 and I got absolutely slaughtered by our travelling fans: 'You don't know what you're doing.' I worked out that one of their subs was on more than all my team's wages put together. I was crucified for being beaten by Bristol City who, no disrespect, are ten times the size of Walsall. I'm not saying all the criticism was unjustified, but here's an idea: at the start of the season, they should publish a league table of budgets to show the fans. If you finish above your place in the budget table, you've done very well. If your budget is £2 million and you're finishing behind someone whose budget is £1 million, then you can't expect to keep your job. It's as simple as that. Until fans can see what their team is up against, you won't have the right context to judge how good a job the manager is doing. Better players cost more money and we just didn't have that luxury.

After we had finished one game, I would think something like, 'Right, who do we play next? Shit . . . Barnsley away. The tunnel's behind the goal at Oakwell, that's where our fans are. I'm going to get pelters walking up the tunnel.' That was in my head all week. It was horrible. Having the fans on your back is a crushing experience. We actually beat Barnsley in an FA Cup replay, 2–0 at home. They would be promoted that season but we played well and the praise was flowing for our performance at the post-match press conference. I said, 'That game could probably get me the sack.' Owing to a quirk in the fixture list, we now had five away games on the trot and we weren't a strong team. We drew two and lost two of them before going to Griffin Park to play Brentford in the fifth. They were top six, we were eighteenth and, after only seven minutes one of their strikers went round our goalie and before the ball had rolled into the back of the net, I swear one of the fans behind our goal had already unfurled his 'Merson out' banner. We lost 5–0. So fierce was the abuse for me, the worst of all language delivered with snarling hate, Mum and Dad left at half-time.

I went to see the chairman after the game and said, 'It's probably time.' He was adamant though. 'Don't be silly, Paul,' he said. 'You'll be all right. Don't worry. We'll get a couple of players in. Let's meet up on Monday after training, get a couple of loans in. You've got Scunthorpe at home on Saturday. You'll turn this around.' And that's what we did. On Monday afternoon, we went through a list of possible signings and I left the stadium and called in to see my mate for a haircut on the way home. While I was in the chair, the chief executive rang and asked me to go back to the Bescot for another chat with the chairman. 'You're getting the sack,' my mate said. 'Don't be silly,' I said. 'I tried to resign on Saturday and he wouldn't have it.' When I arrived Jeff hadn't turned up. He was gutted and just didn't want to do it, which left me and the chief exec. 'I think you should resign,' he said. 'We're expecting a riot on Saturday.'

'A riot?' I said. 'Against Scunthorpe? They'll fit all their supporters on a motorbike. I'm not resigning. I'm not running away. You talked me into staying. You're going to have to sack me.'

'You're gone,' he said.

That was my management career finished. What did I learn? Mainly that experience is priceless. I genuinely thought I would be better than I turned out to be. It's my biggest regret in football, because I didn't give myself a chance. It was a great opportunity that I wasted because I was drinking and gambling like a maniac and the pressure fuelled both addictions. I was in denial at the time, of course. Now I'm more disappointed at failing than I was when it happened.

On 6 February 2006, I went straight to the pub with some mates and got pissed. I wouldn't sober up properly for thirteen more years.

13

A LIFELINE

After twenty-two years as a professional footballer, it was over.

I managed one more game before the end, a fortnight after the sack. My mate Mark Cooper asked me to join Tamworth in the Conference on a part-time contract and, because I had always loved playing football and hoped to find the old joy was still there once the pressures of management had been removed, I agreed to go and see how we got on. It was a bad mistake.

I was a few days shy of my thirty-eighth birthday and I hadn't played for two months. Still, he picked me for a home match against Halifax and it was the hardest game I had ever played in. I wasn't fit enough and nothing I tried came off because the forwards weren't running where I would have expected them to run. So you rein yourself in and play the safe ball, which means your quality can't have the impact it would have higher up. Some kids will have seen me play for the first time in that match and their dads might have said on their way to the Lamb Ground, 'Watch Merson. He's good.' Those kids' lasting memory of that game will be, 'Merson's shit.' And that hurts. Every time I played I always thought about creating a good impression on those who had never seen me before. I couldn't because I didn't have the legs to run the game myself or the quality around me to feed off what I could still provide. You can be the best poker player in the world but if you're not being dealt good hands, you won't win. It's no different with football. If you don't have good players around you, winning is impossible. Sergio Agüero will score hatfuls at Barcelona because he will have great team-mates to play with. He'd struggle to score 15 goals at Rotherham. I don't mean this in an arrogant way, but for a player like me it was far easier to play in the Premier League than in League One and, especially, the Conference. The ball comes to you earlier in the top flight which gives you more time on the ball and the strikers can read the flight of the cross and path of the pass either by instinct, reading your body shape or from the drills you've done. The further you go down the leagues, the fewer options you have every time you're on the ball.

I needed the money, though, and I also needed a purpose, so I didn't quit straightaway. I never had a management contract at Walsall. I was still on my playing deal because when they drew one up, I had said to the chairman, 'If you give me a separate deal and it doesn't go well, you'll be paying me for God knows how long.' I didn't get a pay-off, just a couple more months' pay on my playing contract. I wasn't wealthy. I owed thousands in gambling debts, had been through two divorces and had five children under the age of sixteen.

I turned up for Tamworth training on the Tuesday night and it was absolutely chucking it down. It was pointless carrying on in a storm so I walked off halfway through and went to watch Chelsea v Barcelona in the clubhouse. On the Saturday morning, the bus picked me up at a service station on the M6 for the away game at Grays Athletic. It was a long drive to Essex and Mark came down the aisle and said to me, 'You're sub today, Merse. We've got Cambridge United at home next Saturday and I want you to be fresh for that.' I sulked for the whole journey and, when asked by some fans as I walked to the bench before kick-off why I wasn't playing, I regret to say I couldn't hold myself back, pointing to our dug-out: 'You'd better ask that prick there.' We had a player sent off and were 3–0 down at half-time. Mark looked at me early on and said, 'Warm up.' There was no way I was going on. 'Don't you dare,' I said. 'Don't even think about it.'

I didn't say a word to him after the match – which we lost 5–0 – got changed in silence and asked Nicky Summerbee, the former Man City, Sunderland and Bradford winger, who had driven down from the north-west to play for us, to give me a lift back to Birmingham. You're the first to know that you can't do it anymore, and when you can't get a game against Grays, it's time to face up to the truth.

Weirdly, I could have come back two leagues higher up. My successor at Walsall, Kevan Broadhurst, had found it as tough as me, tougher in fact. He was in charge for 14 games, won one, drew six, lost seven. So it wasn't just down to me. Midway through that run, Jeff Bonser rang me up.

He was still paying me and said, 'Please come back and play.' I really liked Jeff, but I just couldn't do it. 'I can't have been their manager and then sit in the corner as one of the lads,' I said. 'It's not right for me and it wouldn't be right for Kevan.' Sadly, they were relegated to League Two in bottom place. They appointed Richard Money, a coach and manager with experience gathered from jobs in England, Sweden and Australia. He did really well and I was delighted when they were promoted back to League One at the first attempt. That was their level. They were out of their depth in the Championship and trying to do anything but survive in League One. Because of my addictions, so was I.

There was no doubt that I got the manager's job at Walsall because of my name; plus, I was the convenient choice and the chairman liked me. You get one shot at it, and that was mine. I wasn't silly enough to think there was a way back into management for me. The problem was, though, that I was thirty-eight and had not worked outside the game for one minute in my entire life. I was also in the grip of alcoholism and the gambling compulsion was burning hotter than ever.

•

Sky threw me a lifeline in May 2006 when they invited me to Paris as one of the punditry team in the studio for the Champions League final. Had Arsenal lost in the semifinal against Villarreal and Kolo Touré not scored the winning goal, my life could have been so different, definitely unhappier, possibly shorter. Without Sky, I dread to think what a dyslexic thirty-eight-year-old who had just been sacked as the manager of League One Walsall and couldn't play anymore would have done. What *would* I have done? Thankfully, I don't have to dwell on it. Arsenal went through to play Barcelona at Stade de France and that was me on the first rung of the ladder.

I must have done all right, because from there I was asked to do a couple of midweek specials and then invited to fill in on *Soccer Saturday* once a month, then twice a month. I was insecure about damaging my chances of staying on the show because of my difficulty with players' names from the start. I'm not ashamed to admit my dyslexia. I can laugh at myself. I don't get embarrassed, because it's part of who I am and that's the way it is. In life, if people don't like it or want to laugh at me that's their problem, not mine. But I understood that it could be a huge problem in broadcasting if I kept messing up the names. It's why I can't do co-commentary. You wouldn't last one minute, nor deserve to, if you made mistakes saying the names. After only a couple of weeks I rang the producer, Ian Condon, to ask him what I should do. I suggested having some elocution coaching, going to classes to try to learn the names and pronunciations by rote. I would do what it took to make a success of it. And he said, 'One hundred per cent no. You just be yourself on the show. You be *you*. People relate to you, the way you are.' That was music to my ears. Sky haven't tried to change me one bit. That was brilliant for me, a massive thing to get that vote of confidence. I've just been natural on there ever since.

I was appearing more frequently and soon became a regular. I was never offered a contract, though. The head of sport at the time would give me work all day long as a free-lancer, but I know he thought, 'Don't give him a contract, he'll fuck up soon.' They didn't want to be tied to me. Of course, I understood it at the time. I was disappointed but could not fault their reasoning. But when Barney Francis took over as the top man, he called me and said, 'We've decided to give you a contract.' It was one of the best things that has ever happened to me, for him to say he believed in me and trusted me not to let him down. And I never have. But the boost something like that gives someone like me, with my doubts and fears, the lack of self-esteem during and after a binge, was amazing. Things like that, when you feel alone and worthless, are rays of light.

I will always appreciate what Sky and everybody who has worked there have done for me. Earlier, I didn't use that word 'lifeline' lightly. And I hope they know that.

I think I'll be able to say when Sky get rid of me that none of the people behind the scenes, from camera people to make-up staff, floor managers and the guys on security, would say, 'What an arrogant pig he was.' I have a slogan on one of my sweatshirts that reads, 'In a world where you can be anything, be kind.' I have always tried to stick by that, even in the depths of an addictive episode. I could be dying inside, dying, but I would still be polite to people, give them time. I've been in the spotlight all my adult life, since I became an Arsenal regular in my late teens, and people have been asking me for autographs and photographs, a quick chat, for thirty-five years. It's the norm. *I* didn't make me famous, other people did that. People will judge you in the long run not on how good a footballer you are, but how good a person you are. I'd rather people said, 'What a nice person Paul Merson was . . . he was a decent bloke' than 'He was a great player but a tosspot.'

Fifteen years on *Soccer Saturday* have flown by. In my life, as you know, there have been parts when it has been horrible. With all my jobs, bar that little spell at Walsall, it has never seemed like work because I've enjoyed everything I've done. I am so grateful to Sky. I played all my life but working for them has meant I never really missed playing because our *Soccer Saturday* team replicates the camaraderie of the game. We have such a strong bond and rely on each other.

I'd known Charlie Nicholas since I was sixteen, Matt Le Tissier almost as long and Phil Thompson, Chris Kamara and Jeff Stelling have become very close friends. In my drinking days, we used to meet up on a Friday night at a hotel – me, Charlie, Tommo, Kammy and Jeff – and we would have a few drinks and talk about football. The show itself is all off the cuff. Jeff obviously knows the running order but we don't know the questions or in which way the conversation will head. Jeff had this remarkable ability to pick up on something valuable you had said on the Friday night and get you to run with it on the Saturday when you might have forgotten you'd ever said it.

We'd have a good drink until late, but in the morning Jeff would have to get up much earlier than us and go into the office to get the show together. Me, Kammy and Charlie would always meet at nine o'clock for a sauna and a steam. We would say to each other, 'He's had it today. He's bound to be knackered. No way will he be able to do that job for six hours. Today's the day he will struggle.' We've had a nice steam and sauna, showered, changed and had a leisurely breakfast before getting a car to the studios. We would walk into the office and he would put his head up and shake it and exhale as if he was saying, 'I'm rough.' Yes, this is the day, we thought. And then all of a sudden, you go through make-up, into the studio, right on 12 o'clock the music starts and it's 'Here we go'. You would think he was a different person. Honestly, for six hours, it's bang, bang, bang from him. I've never seen anyone like him. Some fools have said about Jeff that anybody can do it. You can't. It's impossible. He goes for six hours and doesn't say 'erm' once. In fifteen years I've never heard him lost for words. It's phenomenal. He is so sharp because his brain is like a sponge. Mine's the other way round. My mind gets rid of everything, his soaks everything up.

At 12 o'clock, the adrenaline starts pumping and the one thing that used to do to me is make me starving. Years ago at Arsenal, on the way home from away trips, we used to have eating competitions. We would have waiter service on the coach, a three-course meal and we would keep the afters or even a full second dinner coming until one of us won. It was always Steve Bould. Not an ounce of fat on him but he could put it away like no one else. I could have run him close at Sky, though. In the studio on *Soccer Saturday* I could have soup, a curry, a bowl of chips, a Mars bar, sandwiches, a couple of bags of crisps, a packet of Revels and all washed down with Red Bull. Tiss would be the same. List everything I ate during those afternoons and serve it up at home and I'd never want to eat it, let alone be able to get it down. No wonder we lost kilos on *Harry's Heroes*. All we had to do was cut out Saturday afternoon's 8,000 calories and the weight dropped off us.

We had such fun and, given the comments we used to get, I think we managed to convey that to the audience. I think I have the greatest job in the world. But in the summer of 2020 when Charlie, Tommo and Tiss were released, it completely terrified me. I'm a one-trick pony. *Soccer Saturday* was made for me and it's the one place on telly where I think my dyslexia is accepted. The programme started years ago and has changed and developed over time. I know nothing's forever but to go from thinking to myself, 'I've got a secure job on a great and very successful show' to the three lads leaving, frightened the life out of me. The day I got the call, all I could think was, 'If I get the sack in a year's time, what am I going to do? I've got nothing.' I didn't feel so desperate the day before and I have to bring myself back to, 'Come on, Paul. Today you've got a job. Don't worry about next year.' That's how I've learnt to cope with life, but it's not my first reaction. That was, and might always be, 'Shit . . . I'd better go out and win as much as I can because I won't be working soon.' That's the madness of the compulsion and what I have to resist.

I was gutted for my friends, like the line from the song – 'we'd been together many a good year'. People might ask, 'Why didn't Paul Merson resign in solidarity?' Well, first off, I have to feed my wife and kids. It's my job. I'm not a multimillionaire who could do that even if I wanted to, but again we come back to football and the 'here today, gone tomorrow' nature of our lives in the game. When a manager is fired, every player doesn't leave the club. David Rocastle was heartbroken to be sold by Arsenal to Leeds in 1992. He was utterly destroyed. We loved that man and yet we didn't all go and ask to leave. Jeff, Kammy, Tommo, Charlie and Tiss made me comfortable being the person I am, as did the whole company. I was scared when the three of them went – I was fifty-two and not stupid. It could easily have been me. I miss them, but the show is evolving all the time, from George Best, Frank McLintock and Rodney Marsh to us four and all the other lads – Tony Cottee, Alan McInally, Matt Murray and so many others who have contributed.

I was frustrated when a mate of mine rang and asked me, 'Did you see what Alan Brazil has written in the paper about you?' I hadn't read it, so he told me Alan had said, 'Paul Merson, great lad, he's been on our show but I just can't help feeling he only didn't get released from *Soccer Saturday* because of his addictions. Sky would have been worried he'd go off the rails.' Had I been drinking and gambling at the time, my temper would have got the better of me. I would have called him up and said, 'How dare you write that? Listen here you effing so-and-so, don't throw judgment on me, give me a bit of respect that I do know my football and Sky value me.' Even sober I was tempted to do it, but once I'd taken a minute I said to myself, 'It's an opinion, that's all it is. It isn't a fact, just one man's way of thinking. I can't change that by ranting and raving at him. Let it go.' And when you do, it's like the air coming out of a balloon. How you react is crucial. Frustration is normal but acting on it rarely gets you anywhere positive.

Everyone who has come on the show over the past year has done really well and I've enjoyed working with them. We have had the added barrier of the COVID-19 guidelines which means we haven't all been able to sit together in the same studio – Ally McCoist and Kris Boyd do it down the line from Glasgow, and we have screens between whoever's in the line-up on a Saturday, Clinton Morrison, Tim Sherwood, Lee Hendrie, Sue Smith or Glen Johnson. It was nice to be able to pass on the advice I'd been given by 'Condo' to Clinton, who has become a good mate of mine: 'You have to be yourself. You know your football, you have an opinion and you have a great personality. Be you. That's all people want to hear.' When lockdown eases, I hope the Friday nights are brought back. I won't be going anymore and Clinton doesn't drink, but it would be a real shame for the rest of the gang not to have that experience.

I do miss the company of my old pals, and I miss how they used to handle my dyslexia. These days, I'm more nervous about it. When I mess up now I find myself worrying; before, the lads would just laugh at me. They would go, 'What was that? What was that word?' Now when I do it, people don't really react that way. Times are changing and people are scared to laugh at people; instead of relaxing me, it sometimes makes me feel a bit self-conscious. The way I've dealt with it is to laugh at myself. The point being I'm not doing it disrespectfully to the people whose names I find it hard to pronounce, I just can't help it. The letters move around in my head and on the page. I felt more comfortable when the lads would join in because there was an inherent kindness there, which said, 'It's all right. It's okay.' Laughing about it eased the sense that it was a serious issue. I was really pleased that Allan Saint-Maximin was so gracious and funny about it last season when his name came out all jumbled as 'Sam Maximus'. Instead of blasting me for my mistake, he found it funny and tweeted his congratulations on a fine debut to his new Newcastle team-mate, 'Sam'.

People come up to me sometimes and say, 'Oh, my God, you're hilarious on *Soccer Saturday*'. I reply, 'You know I'm not *meant* to be. It's not my job to make you laugh; my job's to give an opinion.' And sometimes I'll get it wrong. Last season, for example, I was wrong about Newcastle United fans, saying I thought their criticism of Steve Bruce and the owner was unfair. I didn't understand everything that Mike Ashley has done over the past twelve years and how the supporters feel about it. Over the course of a few months, I really came to appreciate the situation at the club. And it came from all the abuse I received on the social media platforms. They jumped all over me. Reading some of the bad things said about me, though, began something that has helped me understand the fans' point of view. It wasn't nice being absolutely slaughtered, but when I've replied there have generally been positive conversations. That's been the one good thing about social media. When you get the dialogue going, it can be an education. I wrote back, in a way I thought was right: 'Tell me your opinion. You know, you don't have to call me every name under the sun, because I've said something that you don't agree with.' And many of them have apologised for being so heated. When that happens I always think, 'Fair play.' I might have played 800 games but the fan may have seen their team play 800 times and they have just as strong and valid an opinion as mine.

That's the positive side of social media, when you eventually get to that point where you're conversing. But too often, I will say something and the response will be, 'You're clueless. Talking crap. You back on the bag, you fucking druggie?'

I try not to read them. There's no point, but I'm one of those people who is drawn to others' negative views of me because of that lifelong insecurity off the pitch. If I do a speech at a dinner to 150 people in a room and 149 are creasing up and one's looking at me like I'm a piece of shit, it knocks me sideways. That's the person I focus on. I don't see the 149 who are laughing, I only see him. I think, 'Why don't you like me? What am I doing wrong? Why did you come tonight? You know my story.' One day, someone was staring at me and never cracked a smile. It rattled me. I was going to pull him up afterwards and have a word, but on his way out while I was talking to someone else, he came over and said, 'That was absolutely brilliant. I loved that. Thank you very much, what a lovely evening.' He was just listening and yet all I'd seen was a bloke who obviously couldn't stand me.

If they do slag me off by saying I'm back on drink and drugs, I go back and tell them, 'No I haven't taken drugs in more than twenty-five years and I'm thirty months sober.' I need people to know that. And when they say I've got no clue about football, I will reply, 'Well, it's my opinion. I'm not saying it's right all the time. And it's not wrong all the time. But tell me your opinion and what you think, then.' I'm paid to give an opinion. That's my job. I say what I believe. I don't say what everybody else wants me to say. I don't weigh up what's the right thing to say, thinking if I say the wrong thing people are not going to like me. You won't see me umming and aahing when asked a question or pausing for 30 seconds to work out the best way to sit on the fence. I try to be spontaneous and say what I think. If I'm asked in August who will win the league and who will get relegated, I'll make my picks. If I'm wrong it doesn't really matter, but that's not to say they were not sincere beliefs at the time. I've lost millions, you know. I've been wrong quite a few times.

Gary Neville, Jamie Carragher and Jamie Redknapp would tell you they get things wrong as well sometimes. You can't be scared of getting it wrong. You wouldn't last five minutes if you censored yourself to make sure you're not upsetting anyone. And the opposite is true, too. Before Arsenal played Spurs away during the 2020–21 season, I said on the programme, 'Arsenal will have all the play, Tottenham will win the ball, Kane will pass to Son and it's game over.' I said it on Saturday and that's what happened on the Sunday. But I don't get carried away and go on to Instagram and write, 'Look at me, I told you all' because I know I can't be right all the time.

It's not been long since poor Caroline Flack took her own life and there was a welcome mood change on those platforms and in the press, 'Let's not be evil anymore, let's be kind to people.' They all jumped on the bandwagon. In a month they were back with the insults and threats. I did a piece on telly before Manchester United signed Edinson Cavani saying they should buy Harry Kane because he would score them 20 league goals, something I doubted Anthony Martial could do. A couple of days later, I was looking at Instagram and pressed on a request from someone who wanted to get in touch. This was the message: 'What are you fucking talking about, you piece of white trash? Leave Martial alone or I'll fuck your wife up the arse and throw her body into the canal.' People say go to the police but the abusers always get away with it. No one's ever come up to me in Marks & Spencer's or Lidl and said, 'Merson you're a wanker, you're shit.' No one. But on the internet I've had people saying, 'I hope your kids get cancer.' My boy replied saying, 'Thank you. I'm his son.' That's awful, isn't it? It has to stop.

Look at what they did to Phil Foden and Mason Greenwood when they broke the lockdown rules in Iceland. It was straight back to normal, hammering them from pillar to post: 'They're a disgrace, throw them out. Ban them from the England team for life.' Seriously? They were twenty and nineteen, on the biggest high ever after making their debuts. If they were thirty-two, I could just about forgive the pile-on. No one was out there saying, 'You're young, you made a mistake, it's all right.' I was concerned about their wellbeing. When you're down and taking a kicking like that, it can take you to a very dark place. I'm so pleased they finished the season so strongly, as did Chelsea's Kai Havertz. I worry so much for these kids. Havertz is twenty-one, he's had COVID, come to a new country where, unlike eighteen months ago when his parents could fly over to help him get settled, he's on his own and yet he's being criticised as a waste of money. You can have all the money in the world but he's a kid. I'm fifty-three, I have eight children and I still need to talk to my mum and dad all the time.

When I do dinners and we get to the Q&A afterwards, the first question you can usually guarantee is 'How do these players get all this money? It's a joke.' They're entertainers. You don't have a go at Tom Cruise who gets £50 million a film yet has never won an Oscar. No one moans about movie stars and yet wages are always used to beat footballers. It's such a cop out, an excuse to justify these mean attacks. I can't always stick to it myself, but my tip to young players is steer clear of social media. There's nothing to be gained from it – the negativity outweighs any positives. If you don't like criticism and abuse, don't go on it because it will only damage the way you feel.

When I get something wrong, I do now try to make amends. Jeff said to me in 2019: 'What do you think about Harry Maguire?' And I said, 'Not worth the money. Not good enough.' I went too far because he can play, he's comfortable on the ball. I just didn't think he was an £80 million player. When I got home I thought: 'That wasn't right. I shouldn't have said that.' I have no ego problem with admitting a mistake. So I called Brendan Rodgers to get Harry Maguire's number and rang Harry to apologise. I said, 'I'm sorry. I don't agree with the fee but that's not your problem and I want to apologise for saying things which weren't fair.' Harry was surprised to hear from me, thanked me for being so honest and we had a good chat. The only downside is that my son, Freddie, knowing I spoke to the Manchester United captain, keeps saying to me, 'Dad, let's FaceTime Harry Maguire!' When I was gambling I wouldn't have given a flying fuck about upsetting a footballer. Now I'm clean, if I think I've gone over the top, it does bother me.

I also accept that opinions or allegiances will divide people. Sometimes, half the people will love you and the other half will hate you. Jeff Stelling is one of the nicest,

warmest blokes you will ever meet and he's loved everywhere . . . but he's not loved in Darlington because he's from
neighbouring Hartlepool and a massive fan of his hometown
team. He's really no different in one place than the other,
but that's football. Another thing: I don't try to be clever. I
did say to Tiss jokingly when he was sacked, and he'd been
on social media about the lockdown, 'Sometimes it's not
clever to be clever.' That's where I have an advantage. I'm
not that clever and I'm not going to lie. I'm not involved in
politics. When I'm interviewed and they want to talk about
something other than football or addiction I'll say, 'I can't
talk about that. I don't know enough about it.' All I know
is football, all I spend my time talking about is football. I
live it. I watch dozens of games every week. I'm confident
that I can sit down with anybody and talk about football
and can hold my own. I'm not clever enough to use fancy
phrases and I don't have a lot of words in my vocabulary.
I say 'whatsaname' and 'thing' when I can't find the right
word quickly enough. Sometimes, I watch people on the
telly talking about football and think, 'You've lost me at the
roundabout. What word is that?' That's helped me because
I talk to the bloke in the pub. Maybe those people relate to
me because I talk like them, with no airs or graces. It's like
when I started playing: I was living the life of the supporter
in the North Bank, apart from what I was doing in front of
thirty-odd thousand people a week. I'm one of them.

Work has always been the safest environment for me.
When I started gambling again at Middlesbrough in 1998,

for the following twenty years I was always looking for easy money to fuel the habit, not as a way to ease my way into retirement. My family and work have been the salvation of me. I'm always keen to do as much as I can, put the midweek dates in the diary, go in every day over Christmas. Sky's support has meant the world to me and definitely helped pull me back from the brink. 'Jack the Lad' is no more. As far as work and family goes 'lucky lad' is far more appropriate.

14

COMING BACK TO ME

When I started working with Sky, I was on screen once or twice a month. What does an alcoholic, compulsive gambler do from Monday to Friday when he only has to work on Saturdays? I lived in a flat on my own, around the corner from my second wife and had the twins two days a week. On the other days I would ring mates up at 11 a.m. and ask, 'You out today?'

'I can come out for an hour.'

'Don't worry. No point.' I'd move on to the next person, searching around for a friend who could come out for a proper drink until I had found one. And then I'd sit in the pub for hours, come home when it shut, get a Chinese takeaway on the way back and eat it in front of the telly, punting on American sports. I would get up the next day, think 'Did I win or did I lose?', clear up, have a shower and go again. It was an absolute waste of a life, going nowhere.

Away from the children and work, I was numb all the time. I knew I had a mole in the middle of my back for ages that looked strange. It was in a place that was just out of reach if I put an arm over my shoulder or went the other way up the back, right in the gap where you can't apply lotion to yourself. I worshipped the sun, always loved sunbathing and sunbeds, thinking a tan would make me feel good. Wrong again. I ignored the mole for a long time until we were in Orlando on holiday in 2012 and playing golf. One of the kids asked what the mark was on the back of my white T-shirt and it turned out to be blood. When I got home, it got bigger and bigger and I mentioned it to Dr Rogers, who was Walsall's club doctor. We had remained good friends after I was sacked and he kept asking me to come in and have it checked. Eventually I did and they took a biopsy.

I had just pulled into Hartlepool before a benefit dinner I was doing for the football club on behalf of Jeff Stelling when I got the call to tell me it was a melanoma and I needed to have surgery the next day. I just thought, 'That's it. I'm done.' If diagnosed early, skin cancer is very treatable. If you don't get it early, it's one of the worst of all cancers to have because it can quickly spread anywhere. I hadn't gone in to have it looked at as soon as I was aware of it, so this was very late. I was so down in my life that there was no sense of urgency and I didn't worry much once I knew what it was, because I didn't really care about living. I went into surgery the following day and they cut it out. I had fifty stitches. I was so fatalistic about it all that I went into work later the same day to do the *Fantasy Football* show on Sky.

The only thing I was sweating on was someone coming up and slapping me on the back with the fifty stitches because it was agony. But other concerns? None. There was no fear. I'd given up by then. I was living on my own in a flat and just had this devil-may-care attitude. It wasn't that I wanted to die. I was just resigned to whatever fate hit me with. Now I'm happy, I'm petrified about dying. Five years ago, I was diagnosed with diverticulitis, inflammation in the intestines, and when it flares up it's a nightmare, really painful. I panic a lot at the thought that it will get worse. But back then, cancer didn't bother me one iota. I didn't like my life anyway. Doing what I was doing, gambling, drinking, it was just grinding my spirit into the ground. It's really sad my attitude was like that, because plenty of people tragically don't survive skin cancer.

I had to have two scans a year, for five years. Once I had met Kate, I did start to worry that it would come back, thinking before an appointment, 'My life could be turned upside down today.' It never was because, although they laid it on the line for me how foolish I had been to leave it so long, they got it all out. I have never taken my T-shirt off on holiday since, even in the pool. I've become really keen on spreading the word about the dangers of sunbathing. The specialist told me that sunbeds are the worst thing imaginable and said if there was one message you could get across to people, that was it. I come from a generation of people who, the moment they arrive at their hotel on holiday, would throw their bags in the room, put their trunks on and hit the pool. No thought about sun cream. Now when you go into Boots they have everything from oil to 100 SPF, which is like putting a coat on, but I wonder if people my age have all understood the risks because I certainly didn't, not until it actually happened to me. I cringe when I see a builder on a roof in the summer, with no top on. What chance is there of him having cream on his back? Would he ask one of his mates to rub it into that spot where my melanoma was? Look at how many people pass away from it. I didn't appreciate it at the time but I was so lucky.

•

From the day I left Walsall until January 2019 when I had my last drink, the shape of my life was defined by addiction. It was much worse when I was living on my own. My routine changed when I met Kate and moved back down south, but broadly that's how most of my non-working days panned out. I wasn't getting up in the morning and having a drink, but I would go out and binge. I could fairly easily go three or four days without alcohol, no problem, but as soon as I had a drink I was all-in.

When you're an alcoholic and you relapse, there's no enjoyment to the drinking. You haven't forgotten what you are. There's a desperation to it. 'It must be 12 o'clock somewhere' was my great saying. That was the justification, driven by 'Poor, Paul' self-pity. 'Everybody's at it, so why not me?' You try all sorts of ways of convincing yourself that a new approach will bring different results. 'I know, I haven't been a whisky drinker before. I'll drink only whisky.' When that had the inevitable effect, I'd think, 'Hmm, maybe gin?' or 'What if I only drank really nice wine?' 'Wine lover' has got a ring to it, hasn't it? A bit better than 'wino' or 'alco-holic'. Towards the end when my son Freddie and daughter Sienna were very small, I thought I was being disciplined by saying, 'I'll wait until the kids are asleep.' And then I'd reward myself by cracking open a bottle but with the same outcome, waking up on the sofa at 3.30 a.m. with three or four bottles of wine gone, thinking, 'How did that happen?' I was putting a glass to my mouth just for the sake of it.

When I look back now, sober, I just think, 'My God, what a waste of time.' I've talked about what it cost me in terms of mental health, family and money but there are loads of less important things too, loads of experiences I've missed out on. I've been all around the world, gone to places most people could only ever dream of visiting and never got fur-ther than the bar in the hotel. You know that cliché about players going to Beijing on tour but they couldn't be arsed to leave a card game or a drinking session to see the Great Wall of China? That was me. As soon as I had that first drink of the day, that was the end of the day as far as productivity or sensitivity to others went. It wouldn't matter what country I was in, once I started there was no moving me. There's a bit in the second series of *Harry's Heroes* when I had stopped drinking and Harry took a few of us to the Eiffel Tower. In my boozing days, I wouldn't have bothered. I'd have been on a barstool. Sightseeing for me was the bottom of a glass and a betting app on my phone.

I could have been on *Top of the Pops* when Arsenal per-formed 'Shouting for the Gunners', our 1993 FA Cup final song. It's a minor thing compared with the rest of the opportunities I've wasted, but that was a big deal in those days. We all met up in a pub beforehand and when the bus came to take everyone else to the studio, I stayed behind to carry on drinking. I had to tell my wife that David Seaman and Tony Adams had blocked the cameras' view of me.

The twelve years before I'd had enough and went back to Alcoholics Anonymous are a long time. There are hundreds of episodes of drinking I could recount, but to do so would be pointless because they're all basically the same. When you're young and going out it's a laugh – all lads together, playing football, getting pissed. It's great. But when it takes over your life, it's boring. The addictions turn you into such a selfish person. I was particularly precious about Sundays even after moving back down south and marrying Kate. I looked at it as, 'I worked Saturday so Sunday is *my* day.' I might play football in the morning for a veterans' side and then I'd go to the pub up the road at noon, make sure my phone was fully charged and take a charger with me as well. I would sit on a stool, staring at my phone. I would sit there drinking and gambling away on my own in a pub that was packed. I was there but not there. If I fancied company, there were some nice regulars. I would drink with anyone. Alcohol gets rid of the shyness and the advantage of being well-known is you never have to make the first move, people will always come up to you to talk about football. It didn't matter who I was with, though. I only had eyes for the phone.

It was drinking for the sake of drinking, really. At first, I'd start off at twelve and get home at six but then carry on drinking indoors. For a few weeks I was fine sticking to that routine, but by the time it got to three or four months, then I was in from opening time until it shut, 11 hours of drinking. Six o'clock would turn to seven, then a couple of weeks later I'd go home at eight. Soon, I would be ringing up at eight and saying, 'I'll be another half hour', then I wouldn't answer the phone. If I'd have said to my wife, 'I'll be home at nine' and was, it wouldn't be a problem. But when you start by saying, 'I'll be there at six' and you're not back, and not answering her calls at ten, the selfishness is off the scale. I would come home and Kate would say, 'You must have been having a good time?' And more often than not I'd say, 'No'. My mood was entirely dependent on the gambling. If I'd won, I'd laugh and joke with people, get up on to a table and join in singing 'Sweet Caroline'. If I hadn't won, I'd sit at the bar, miserable, chasing my losses.

The compulsion wants you to itself, even when you're not physically alone. I'd be watching Freddie on the PlayStation and all Kate could hear coming from the room is our son saying, 'Please stop looking at your phone, Dad.' As soon as I would start gambling I'd tell myself, 'Right, don't look at your phone for 10 minutes to check the score. But I'd look at it ten times in one minute. In your head, you're telling yourself, 'Don't look, don't look.' And you can't help but look. It's madness. You've got your voice in your own head begging, 'Please don't look' and you're ignoring it and looking every six seconds. Every time we went out for a meal, I would put my phone face up on the table and look at it constantly. My wife would eventually say, 'How do you think that makes me feel?' I thought I was being quite subtle. When we went out with friends I could be sitting around a table with ten people and I'd be staring at my phone. She'd tell me, 'It's embarrassing, people are talking to you and you're not even listening. People are telling you things four times and you're not taking any notice.' I wasn't really there. I would be in a room of people and wouldn't have a clue what was going on. I was off in that other world.

Even worse than that, though, were the mood swings, the terrible volatility.

The kids could be in the bath one day when I'd won a right few quid and they would be splashing me and laughing. I would be joining in, everything's funny and we would have a great time. Two days later, I could have done all my money and they would splash me and I'd shout, 'What are you doing? What are you splashing me for?' They're little kids and it was funny a couple of days ago and, of course, they think it's going to be the same again. I was so up and down all the time.

When you're winning you either don't go to bed or you fly out of bed at four in the morning because you can't wait to go again and there's always something to bet on and watch. Phil Thompson used to say to me when we arrived at the *Soccer Saturday* studio, 'What've you been on this morning, Merse?' And I might say, 'Well, I started off in

New Zealand on a Super 15s rugby union game at 4 a.m., then moved to Australia for a bit of rugby league and then some Aussie Rules.' I would study up on those sports so I would know as much as I could about the players and form. Laughing about it with the lads was an ego thing. I'd have Thommo in stitches, but it was no fun because what I didn't tell him was that the moment one match finished, I would have to bet on something else. I couldn't wait half an hour. I could have done all my money for the week before they were even awake. They didn't know that because, win or lose, I would clown about.

I've been to Florida maybe thirty times on holiday. I would play with the kids in the morning and at one o'clock I would go and get my first drink and that was me off duty for the day, doing nothing but pure drinking. I'd started so I'd finish, seeing this drunkenness out to the bitter end. I would always say we went there because the kids enjoyed it so much. The real reason was because I had the basketball and ice hockey which meant I could bet all through the day and night. It wasn't for the kids to go to Disneyworld and see the fresh joy and wonder on each one's face when they saw it for the first time. I would take them but spend, and I'm not joking, not even an hour in there. After the quickest race round I'd say, 'C'mon, let's go' and drag them back to where we were staying. The bar was open and I wanted to be punting. We went there in 2019 when I had stopped drinking and gambling and we spent six hours in Disney. I absolutely loved it, seeing their faces when they caught sight of Mickey Mouse, instead of me stomping around thinking, 'How much longer?' It was the best holiday I've ever had.

It was always me, me, me. Now, seeing the kids happy, taking Freddie to football . . . that's the be-all and end-all for me. The simple things are all I strive for, all I want: to be a good dad, to be there for my wife and children. When Sadie was born in January 2021, I wasn't just there in body but in spirit as well. I was present and engaged. During the last lockdown, I would get up in the morning with Sienna and then go back for Sadie, feed her, help get Sienna ready for school and take her. And when I came back, Kate would be home-schooling Freddie and I would pitch in where I could. I would do it because I genuinely wanted to do it without any other agenda. I used to do it for the brownie points – 'That means I can go to the pub later on, I can sit around and gamble and watch three football matches in a row.' I did want to do it in the past, don't get me wrong, but with a gambler's thinking there's always a goal at the end of it. When I'm not gripped by the compulsion, that bargaining isn't there. I'm only focused on them.

Before, there was not enough room in my head for the things that should have been at the forefront of my thoughts. When I didn't have money, I was exhausted. My mind was on overdrive all day with gambling. 'What am I going to do next? What am I going to bet on tomorrow? How can I get money tomorrow? Who can I ring up that I've paid back quickly enough the last time and will lend me the money again to get a bet on. Then I've got my wages coming on Friday so I can use that to pay him back. That gets me past Tuesday.' That was my brain, every minute of the day, scheming. Just working out frantically, 'I'll bet on this and if that wins, I'll bet on that and if that wins I'm going to bet on that.' All the time. The cost to your dignity is horrible, ringing up or texting people, who haven't earned a twentieth of what you've blown in their lives, asking to borrow money. 'This better not be for gambling,' they might say. 'Course not,' you lie. 'I just got a bill I need to pay.' It's so degrading it eats away at your soul, absolutely kills you inside.

But when you're a compulsive gambler and you have money, it isn't burning a hole in your pocket, it's burning a hole in your mind. It's just dangerous. For a gambler, having money is like being an alcoholic and carrying six cans of lager around in your bag. And not drinking them. Why carry them around? It's the same with money. I'd think, 'Right, I've got some. I need time on my own now to gamble. Don't want to be around my wife and kids.' So I would engineer a big argument with Kate, provoke her into saying, 'You might as well leave then.' And I'm, 'Okay, see you, bye.' Then I would go round the corner to our old flat which we've kept, sit there for two days of madness, of constant drinking and gambling until it had all gone. It's such a selfish thing. It takes over. When it's on them, the addict only cares about the addiction. I'm so far from that as a person it's unreal. I worry about people more than I worry about myself. I hope everybody's all right. I haven't got enemies or would wish anything bad to happen to anyone. I always want people to do well. But when you're gambling, all you're worried about is yourself. I like being a caring person but you see yourself just making your wife unhappy, your kids unhappy, yourself unhappy and you just can't stop. This cycle went on for years. I liken it to an old, scratched LP going round and round that record player because it keeps jumping back to the start before it ever ends. It's the same old routine time after time.

When I look back at it now with a clear head – and that's not every day, occasionally the clarity goes and the temptation all but overpowers my judgement – the realisation that I never stood a chance is glaring. Yes, I know that the compulsion is about the process of betting, rather than the money, so I could never win in the long-term. If I had won a million, I would have only tried to double it. There is no end point other than being broke. That's the only time a binge stops. As long as you've got some money or credit, it will last until it runs out. But, in addition to that is the sheer exploitation of the compulsive gambler by the industry, licensed and unlicensed.

Let's be frank, things have changed for the better. There's more awareness, more checks, limits and ways to protect yourself, many of them relying on self-referral, which has not been much use to me. To those who say, 'you were a consenting adult and you should have known better', I would concede that when the addict isn't betting he *does* know better. But the moment the compulsion's on them, common sense goes out of the window. When they ring to check if you really mean to have five grand on the evening match, which gambler with the compulsive fever raging is going to say, 'Actually, now you mention it, no'? So they take the bet. Giving someone like me 100 grand credit is like abusing me. Over the years, they have skinned me of my money. All they had to do is look at my credit account activity, check I could afford the losses by asking to see my bank account and shutting me down when they found out I had nothing to play with, never mind 100 grand. Instead I was borrowing money to feed my addiction, it has all flowed into their profits and I'm still paying it off. The natural instinct of the gambler is to win their losses back, so when you get care calls saying, 'You've lost 100 grand, are you sure you're all right?', what else are you going to say, other than, 'Of course, can I get another bet on?' If you say no, they'll close you down and then how are you ever going to win your money back? You have to keep ploughing it in. They don't do that before or tell you they think you're a problem gambler and they're going to close your account until after you've lost huge amounts. It's never before or during, only ever after the event. Okay, if they think I'm a problem gambler, why don't they give me my money back then? What changed over the past six months? If you're a problem gambler, you're a problem gambler. The bets have stayed the same. They didn't start off at 2p and now they're twenty grand. It's take, take, take solid for six months and then they tell you that you have a problem. Actions are stronger than words. It enrages me to think they kept taking all those years.

To be fair, one or two private bookies have sussed straight off that I'm not well by the scale of the bet I tried to get on and have said, 'No, you're not right. I don't want to know.' In general, though, private bookies have a different style to the corporations but it's the same outcome 'Why bet with them?' you may ask if you're not a gambler. For a start, you can usually get more money on. You go into a betting shop and try to put three grand on a 1–3 shot, and they won't take it. Bet on the high street and win big and they'll try to tell you there's a ceiling to what they'll pay, argue it out and, when you've got whatever winnings they're entitled to give you, close you down. It's how they operate. When you win with a private bookie, they drag it out: 'I'll get it in a couple of days for you.' They know full well that you're not capable of sitting there for three days without having a bet. They know. Years ago at Walsall during the binge when I drained my pension fund, I was betting with a firm whose settling up terms were at the end of the month. I rang them on a Friday because I was 100 grand up and wanted to bank it. 'Can you wait until Monday? We'll sort it then.' By Monday morning I owed *them* 100 grand. They rang me first thing threatening all sorts if I didn't pay up immediately. I hadn't threatened them on Friday when *they* owed me. The threatening isn't the point. It's the exploitation. They know what I am better than I do when the fog of compulsion clouds my brain. I'm not a human being to them. I'm a fucking cash machine.

•

After twelve years of denial, of soaring, brief highs and long, punch-drunk, lows, of constant anxiety and inner turmoil, the thing that made me see my addictions for what they are, the damage they do to me rather than to other people, was a telly programme. 'Oh, I ain't that bad,' I would always say . . . until I had that rarest of opportunities to see myself and my life through my own eyes. That was obviously never the intention of *Harry's Heroes: The Full English*. It was supposed to be an entertainment show, a vehicle for Harry Redknapp, using his brilliant man-management skills, to try to coax a bunch of forty- or fifty-something England players back to fitness to play a one-off match against Germany's veterans.

The fear I had when approached was how they planned on putting it together, whether they were going to make us look silly, play up the booze and the weight and the old legs. But Harry and the quality of players already on board convinced me to sign up. I knew I could handle it physically. I'm fortunate I can still play football. Not at the same standard, obviously, but I can still kick the ball around and run while a lot of the players I played with can hardly move. It couldn't have been done with better lads: Dave Seaman, Rob Lee, Lee Sharpe, Ray Parlour, Neil Ruddock, Mark Wright, Matt Le Tissier, Chris Waddle, Robbie Fowler and Mark Chamberlain. A lot of us had known each other for thirty years or more. We were greyer, bigger and much slower but we all clicked and that natural 'up' dressing-room spirit was rekindled in an instant. It was a perfect mix and what was so good about it was we all had a story to tell, we all had our joys and sadnesses which showed how normal we are. If you had put another manager in charge, it wouldn't have worked. Harry put the jigsaw together and handled us cleverly. He was quite harsh on the voiceover about the state of some of us, but he wasn't like that when we were filming, knowing it wouldn't be constructive to say it out loud when, at the start, a few lads were struggling to breathe, let alone play.

Following the diet, I lost more than a stone, Tiss lost two, but I was still drinking during the first series. They sprang the bleep test on us the morning after I'd gone through a bottle and a half of gin. If I'd known I wouldn't have had a drink, and although swapping gin and vodka for the usual twelve pints of lager helped the weight-loss, it definitely did for me in the bleep test. I still got to seven or eight, though.

None of the series was scripted but they shot loads of footage and it was quite tightly edited. My main set-piece in the programme, when I broke down in the back of a taxi and spoke about the toll gambling had taken on my life and the hole I was in at that particular time, was entirely spontaneous. I was overwhelmed by guilt, debt and hopelessness. I felt I had no control and that I'd had enough but couldn't stop digging deeper and deeper. There were tears and loads of fears. I've been there before but this time I was on national television. They took me to see Drewe Broughton, an ex-pro and counsellor, who had experienced addiction issues of his own, and we spoke, which was helpful. He was a good man but he didn't tell me anything I didn't really know, that compulsive gamblers can never win and that Gamblers Anonymous was the only thing that had worked for me in the past. It was time to go back. For continuity reasons they wanted me to chat to Dave Seaman and Robbie Fowler about 'my gambling hell' a couple of days afterwards but, and this is the rollercoaster of my life, those feelings had gone. I actually felt good that day.

Hitting rock bottom with gambling midway through the series inspired the return to GA. My return to AA would take a little longer. The night before the finale, the game against Germany at Brisbane Road, me and Ray Parlour were in the bar until 4 a.m. He knocked on my hotel room door and said, 'Are you coming down for one?' It's back to Beth in *The Queen's Gambit*, the night before her match against the Russian in Paris. She's me. You've got a massive game the next day and you think, knowing you're an alcoholic, 'Go on, I'll have one.' But I can't have *one*. At 4 a.m. before a big game I've worked twelve weeks for, I was completely paralytic.

Thank God, I was full of running the following evening. I was nervous. Neither Kate nor Freddie had seen me play football. I played well and to have the icing on the cake, to round the keeper and score the winner, was wonderful. It felt like it was meant to be after everything I had been through, a happy ending that wasn't at all contrived. The Germans are not going to let you score in a month of Sundays if they can help it. They were winners and to have that old competitive fire burning at the age of fifty was brilliant, a big thing for me. It was on the telly, saved on Sky+, so Freddie can watch it forever.

Watching it changed my life. When you've been out drinking, you've had far too much and gone back to the pub the following evening, everyone goes, 'You should have seen you last night. You were absolutely rotten.' No one ever films it do they? Same with you on your knees at 2 a.m. with all your savings and borrowings lost after a three-day bender. The memory is in your head but not shoved in your face. When the programme came out in March 2019, it allowed me to see the wreckage my gambling and drinking had left, how powerless I was in front of them. The warm wishes from members of the public, shocked at what addiction had done to me, were an unexpected but uplifting extra.

Seeing it has certainly helped me stay off drink, but it wasn't the tipping point for stopping. In January 2019, Kate showed me a picture she had taken at Freddie's nativity play. I'd given it a swerve to go to the pub. He didn't know that, though. He had expected me to be there and at the end, my wife's photograph captured the moment after he had seen her and was looking round to find where I was. Eager anticipation gave way to confusion and disappointment that his daddy wasn't there. It was heart-breaking and shook me to the core. Regret and shame hit me like a sledgehammer. I didn't want to be that callous, selfish man. I wanted the real me to come back.

That's what sent me back to AA and I haven't had a drink since. This time, I went in for me. I went because I couldn't bear it anymore. It wasn't the FA forcing me into rehab by putting my career on the line, it wasn't the PFA and my chairman taking me at my first word when I was already having second thoughts, and whisking me off to Arizona. It was me, 100 per cent invested in being a better man. Had I carried on drinking, I would be dead by now. I was going nowhere, drinking madly, gambling like a lunatic and when I saw myself acting like that through the camera on the telly, it's no exaggeration to say it saved my life. It was exactly what I needed.

The difference in me between the two series filmed in 2018 and 2019 was like night and day. I wasn't sure about doing *Harry's Heroes: Euro Having A Laugh*. Not many TV sequels have ever been as good as the original but they had a real vision for it and to do it clean and sober was a hell of an experience. A lot of my contribution revolved around my relationship with Neil Ruddock. I've known him since we were seventeen. He's my mate and I really care about him. The state he was in when we went to Paris was me nine months before on the first show, struggling, drinking like crazy, bottling up all the fears and self-hate, and acting the clown. When his wife came over for some filming and they joined a few of the lads in a pub to watch the England game, they would have had the best intentions. But it's the same old story – they have a few drinks and there's no way they're seeing sense now, which is exactly how I would have behaved if I'd still been boozing instead of being in my hotel room. Given his weight and his serious heart condition, when the lads were sending through photos of him, off his trolley with a bra on his head, I was really upset and worried for him. It was flashback time, to me the year before, on the same destructive path, confused, scared, unable to see a way out. You become a tomorrow man: 'I'll pack it in tomorrow.' I put off tomorrow for fourteen years. The end of drinking for me saved my sanity and my life. Because of Razor's health, my biggest fear was he could keel over at any minute, the end of his life would come before the end to the drinking that was killing him.

That's why I confronted him the following morning. As I said on the show, if I didn't care I wouldn't have bothered. Of course, he found it difficult to accept at first. He was hungover, still a bit pissed and he's a proud man. Denial makes you defensive and I wasn't surprised he acted the way he did, getting the hump and storming off. We made up quickly, though. He has told me since that he understood I wasn't doing it because I was so squeaky clean and judgemental after stopping. It came from love. It was powerful TV, strong stuff. I've had addicts come up to me since and say, 'Cor, I wish one of my mates had said that to me.' But it's hard to be honest like that. There must be 100 people who wanted to say to me over the years, 'Fucking hell, Paul. Knock it on the head.' I'm sure they would have thought it wasn't their place to do that. On that day with Neil, I just felt I had to speak because his blood pressure was through the roof and there was very little time left to care whether it was my place or not to tell him. I'm delighted he's doing well now and has lost some weight after the heart op. That's nothing to do with me, you can only do it for yourself. He's got a lovely wife and kid, he's a good, good bloke. Who wants to die at such a young age?

Helping to save two lives is a pretty good return for a show about washed-up footballers, isn't it?

15

LIVING FOR TODAY

My addiction doesn't like me at the moment.

It's as strong as it ever was, but I'm in a good space. The last few weeks have probably been the happiest I've been in my whole life. I have nothing materially. All the money I earned in twenty-two years as a professional footballer, the houses and cars have all gone. But now I understand myself and what drives that destructive behaviour. If I don't feel good today, I don't try to chase it away with a bet or a drink. I'm content just being on an even keel. My life has been an absolute rollercoaster since God knows how long, but now it's flat. That's a massive relief. Being on the level, not chasing highs, not suffering lows, is new for me. It takes some time for the addictive personality to get used to a normal life. When I have a full calendar and I'm busy, everything fits together and life is good. I revel in routine, the job I love, Freddie's football training and matches, the children's swimming lessons, Sienna's Little Gym, being there for the baby, Sadie, and my meetings at GA and AA.

I'm not complacent. I would not dare say I have cracked drinking and will never have another one after thirty months of sobriety. I have surrendered to the addiction, acknowledging I'm powerless to stop once I've started. I tell myself I have an allergy to alcohol. If you were allergic to peanuts, you would never eat another. That's my thinking with alcohol: the next drink could kill me.

With gambling, it is more complicated. I can be around people who are drinking and it doesn't bother me. At the moment it's not about resisting temptation; the temptation isn't there and I'm grateful for that. Today, I'm a million miles from a bet, as far as I've ever been from having a bet, but that's because I can see clearly. It's not always the case. I can't be in the company of people who are gambling or talking about bets. It's a massive trigger for me.

When I talk about wanting to be 'normal', I mean I want to be like the majority of other people because compulsive gambling is normal to me. The addiction is so seductive. Some days it tries to convince me by making points, which appear to be reasonable. It tells me that the only hope of making amends for all the grief, all the losses, even now, is to win the money back. 'I'll win, I'll get on a roll, I'll get my money back. Why can't it be me this time? Why can't I have the luck? Just win £300 a day. How hard can that be?' That's how insidious it is. After all the experiences I've had, the number of times it has beaten me up and left me wanting to die, and the illness can still sound sensible. It takes concentration and sometimes intense effort not to do what it wants me to do.

That's why I need meetings. Hearing people and their

stories helps me remember why it's worth not giving up. Talking is the only therapy that works for me.

Addiction is about changing the way you *feel*, however briefly. And forgetting what it's done to you in the past is the key to its charm. During the first lockdown, I stopped going to virtual GA meetings. I carried on with AA, thinking I could kill two birds with one stone, but the compulsion blindsided me in a moment of vulnerability. Without GA my shield had gone. I had a lot of work in the diary, which for me means I can pay off my loan. I've got a plan I'm working to that enables me to clear my debts *and* save for a house. It was all right at the start and then every week, as my agent rang and added to the list of cancellations, I started to scheme. I had enough money in our savings to make the repayments, but I didn't want to do that. I wanted both to pay the instalments and save for a house. So I used the savings to try to double them up. I lost everything.

I didn't mean to, I never have meant to do all my money. But it's like you're possessed, frantic, flirting with insanity. At the end of the gambling binge, you're just pleased the money's gone, so you don't have to do it anymore.

With drinking, I have reached a stage where I'm not going to drink, because I know when I do, I can't stop. And I don't want to do that. I can rationalise with the addiction before it gets hold of me.

With gambling, when I can't think straight I have yet to reach that rationale before it happens, only after. If the compulsion overwhelms my reason and I relapse, the goal that tricked me back in, double your money, say, lasts about two minutes.

I have won what I went in to win loads of times. Never once have I gone, 'Great, I've done it. I'll stop now. That's helped.' All the winning does is buy the addiction more time to extend the torture, prolong the madness. I simply carry on because the compulsion's goal is to keep me doing things I don't want to do until it's driven me to destruction. In those moments, losing everything is the only freedom from it. You can't feed the bastard if you've got no money left. It's like the counsellor in Arizona said all those years ago: it's trying to kill me and who's to say the next bet isn't going to be the one that sends me over the edge?

It might be in five years, ten years or thirty years when it tries to work its way between my earholes again. It's persistent. It won't accept that it's beaten, because it never truly can be, only managed, mentally and physically by me only having pocket money these days. I don't know how many comebacks I have left. Each relapse in the past had taken a bigger psychological toll than the previous one.

It really is that serious. That's what I hold at bay all the time with meetings and the understanding of my family. Talking about it really helps. Having people listen and understand without doubting your sincerity is the key to getting well. Piers Morgan has said some shitty things in the past, but he's an intelligent bloke. Yet when he said Meghan Markle was lying when she spoke about her struggles with poor mental health, that was the worst thing anyone could ever say. It could make one person think, 'I can't say anything. If they're calling out Meghan Markle, what are they going to do to me? Call me a liar?' To me, the concept of Mental Health Awareness week is a joke. It's not something you can contain in seven days and then put away for twelve months while you go back to your old ways of judging people, talking about 'strength' and 'weakness' and personal choice. It has to be a lifelong campaign to educate people about the illnesses of depression, anxiety, insecurity and the addictions they trigger.

You don't want people bottling it all up. That's how I used to be and it wrecked my life for years. Talking without embarrassment about the darkness of addiction and depression, without fear of being condemned, has saved me. This book is part of that process, trying to help me and everyone else understand the everyday realities of what addiction does to the addict and the people in their lives.

We have to find a way of living with our enemy. Today, I can cope by breaking down my life into the bits between picking my head up off the pillow and laying it down again at night. Every morning I tell myself, 'Live in the day.' I have always loved John Lennon's 'Imagine'. I know most people see it as his political vision, but to me it begins as a song about dealing with addiction by a man clearly in recovery. Every line rings true but none more so than, *Imagine all the people, living for today.* That's how the recovering addict must approach the rest of their lives.

A mobile phone has not always been my friend, but now I have this screensaver I look at every morning when I make my first coffee. It's called Two Golden Days:

> *There are two golden days about which I never worry:*
>   *yesterday and tomorrow.*
> *Those days belong to God, therefore that leaves me*
>   *only today.*
> *Any man can fight the battle of just one day.*
> *Old friend, it is only when we have the burden of those*
>   *two awful eternities, yesterday and tomorrow,*
>   *that we will break down.*
> *Those days are God's days, leave them with him.*
> *Therefore, I will journey just one day at a time.*

You don't have to find that spiritual side comforting to get the message: one day at a time is the road to rescue.

I have so many blessings: my wonderful children, the best job in the world, a wife and family who understand me and my illness. Kate's mother has experience of gambling addiction in the family and her empathy and support have been a massive help to Kate in her accepting that I wasn't a terrible person when I've lost money, I'm still the man she loves. You can hate the illness and love the person.

If there's one message I hope you can take from this book, it's that: *hate the illness, love the person.* And if my story helps one person, an addict or a member of their family, to recognise themselves and gives them hope, it will be the biggest achievement of my life. All the best things I've already done came down to teamwork and this is no different. Family, obviously, is most important and the meetings are an arena in which you can empty yourself of all your darkest fears to an army of people in recovery who are on your side. I also have a good friend I talk to every day without fail. I send him a text in the morning, 'How are you, how's the head today?' And he does the same for me.

In recovery, you give and receive. Talking wears the addiction down. It doesn't want you communicating with anyone else. It wants you to feel boredom, shame, self-hatred, greed and a cynical indifference to your fate.

Always remember, it needs you on your own.

But it doesn't have to be that way. You are not alone.

Acknowledgements

A massive thank you to everyone who has helped me put this book together and to everyone who has supported me down the years.

To my mum and dad, and to Louise, Keith and Gary.

To Kate and all the kids – thanks for the great memories, even when I wasn't well. And to Kate's mum and dad, Kay and Pete.

To Condo, Jeff Stelling, Matt Le Tissier, Phil Thompson and Charlie Nicholas – thanks for always making me feel so welcome and comfortable.

To all the gang at Sky Sports for their support, and especially to Barney Francis and Gary Hughes for believing in me.

To Gene – thank you for everything you've done over the last few years.

To Niall, Simon, Rob and Luke – thanks for helping in my recovery.

To my ghost writer Rob Bagchi, for his patience and perseverance, and for helping me capture so well exactly what I wanted to say.

To Jonathan Taylor, Tom Whiting and the top-drawer team at Headline for giving me the opportunity to publish this book.

Index

INDEX

INDEX

INDEX

INDEX

INDEX

INDEX

INDEX